Rev'd
6/13

WM458

ANZR/1

WM,458

UNIVERSITY OF PLYMOUTH
LIBRARY SERVICES

MELANIE

Klein

STAFF LIBRARY
ST. LAWRENCE'S HOSPITAL
BODMIN
PL31 2QT

D0263574

Key Figures in Counselling and Psychotherapy

Series editor: Windy Dryden

The *Key Figures in Counselling and Psychotherapy* series of books provides a concise, accessible introduction to the lives, contributions and influence of the leading innovators whose theoretical and practical work has had a profound impact on counselling and psychotherapy. The series includes comprehensive overviews of:

Sigmund Freud
by Michael Jacobs

Melanie Klein
by Julia Segal

Eric Berne
by Ian Stewart

Carl Rogers
by Brian Thorne

MELANIE

Klein

Julia Segal

STAFF LIBRARY
ST. LAWRENCE'S HOSPITAL
BODMIN
PL31 2QT

SAGE Publications
London • Newbury Park • New Delhi

© Julia Segal, 1992

First published 1992, Reprinted 1993

All rights reserved. No part of this publication may be
reproduced, stored in a retrieval system, transmitted or
utilized in any form or by any means, electronic,
mechanical, photocopying, recording or otherwise, without
permission in writing from the Publishers.

SAGE Publications Ltd
6 Bonhill Street
London EC2A 4PU

SAGE Publications Inc
2455 Teller Road
Newbury Park, California 91320

SAGE Publications India Pvt Ltd
32, M-Block Market
Greater Kailash – I
New Delhi 110 048

British Library Cataloguing in Publication Data

Segal, Julia
  Melanie Klein. – (Key Figures in
  Counselling & Psychotherapy Series)
  I. Title   II. Series
  150.195

  ISBN 0–8039–8476–6
  ISBN 0–8039–8477–4 (pbk)

Library of Congress catalog card number 92–056710

Typeset by Mayhew Typesetting, Rhayader, Powys
Printed in Great Britain by J. W. Arrowsmith Ltd, Bristol

Contents

Acknowledgements

I am indebted to the Wellcome Institute for the History of Medicine for access to the Melanie Klein Archives and to the Melanie Klein Trust for permission to quote from Klein's books. I am grateful to Hanna Segal, not only for permission to quote from her book, but also for her suggestions for revisions to this one. It is first and foremost to her that I owe my interest in Klein. I am also grateful to Ruth Malcolm; Windy Dryden directed, encouraged and asked pertinent questions with his usual skill; Susan Worsey gave excellent editorial back-up. I owe many thanks to Dan for his ruthless editing, as well as for much else in my life. Joel and Paul very kindly kept out of the way, and I apologise to them for 'always working'.

1

The Life of Melanie Klein

Melanie Klein's name has been at the centre of controversies both within the psychoanalytical community and outside it. Her work challenges the assumptions and beliefs both of people who know nothing of psychoanalysis and of those who use it in their work as counsellors, psychotherapists and psychoanalysts.

By the 1920s, when Klein began work, psychoanalysts had developed considerable insight into childhood through their own personal analyses and that of their patients. However, there were few mothers among them. Klein brought the insights of a mother to psychoanalysis: she was able to learn from observing and attempting to analyse her own children in a way few of her colleagues could. Eventually she advised her students strongly against attempting to analyse their own children, but by then the groundwork for understanding children was already laid.

Klein learnt to interpret children's fantasies and play through applying her reading of Freud's work *On Dreams* (1975, vol. 5: 629) and insights from her own analysis. From the analysis of her son at the age of 5, she discovered how deeply children's views of their parents could be distorted by the child's own feelings and how effective analysis of their unconscious ideas and feelings could be. Her experience persuaded her that interpretations of their deepest anxieties could free children's intellectual and fantasy life.

In her unpublished autobiography, Klein relates a story of her father. As a young man he answered a call for doctors in a cholera epidemic. Where other doctors stood at the windows, he entered the cottages and treated the cholera patient as he would any other. This could stand as an allegory for Klein's own work: where others feared to interpret, Klein interpreted the most frightening and disturbing material as she would any other. Where others modified their technique in the face of the anxieties arising from the work, Klein refused to modify hers.

It is perhaps not surprising that some doctors and analysts should have found her work disturbing. As anyone who has worked with children or confused adults will know, following fantasies, beliefs, feelings and thoughts through to their logical conclusion, without drawing back at the unpalatable ones, can be a very disturbing undertaking for the therapist as much as for the client. Even sitting and listening for an hour to very disturbed children or adults can be exhausting and somehow threatening. Klein found that the discomfort could be borne: the patient could obtain relief and the analyst insight. It was this which led to her most far-reaching insights and to the understanding eventually of some of the craziest forms of communication between patient and analyst, as well as to a deepening understanding of normal processes.

Melanie Reizes, Born 1882

Melanie Klein dictated notes for an autobiography which she never finished and which, together with letters, can be read in the Wellcome Trust Archives, London. Phyllis Grosskurth in her biography of Klein (Grosskurth, 1986) provides a rich source of other material. I draw upon Grosskurth's book, though I disagree with many of her interpretations.

Klein's autobiography leaves an impressive picture of her father's early life. Moriz Reizes was born into an orthodox Jewish family but studied to become a doctor against his parent's wishes. He spoke ten languages and was extremely well read. His independence of spirit and his rejection of religious dogma, though not of his family, was something which Klein inherited and kept all her life.

Klein's mother, Libussa Deutsch, was younger than her husband. They were married in 1875, when Moriz was 47 and Libussa 23. Witty and beautiful, with a respect for education which she shared with her husband, she seems to have been deeply involved with household matters and with her children. In her letters before they married she sounds somewhat cowed by her older, highly educated suitor. 'I feel only too clearly,' she wrote to him 'that I will not be able to follow your lofty and enthusiastic flights which keep you in the highest heights, in ever growing, enthusiastic distances. My wings are tied. I am too earthbound even to dare to dream of following you' (Grosskurth, 1986: 7). Her letters to her daughter many years later are full of 'earthbound' reality: household matters, financial difficulties and family news.

Klein thought that her father was totally devoted to her mother, but that her mother did not reciprocate the affection so deeply. Her description of her mother in her autobiography was of an intelligent, lively, courageous but unassuming woman. 'She has in many ways remained my example . . . I remember the tolerance she had towards people and how she did not like it when my brother and I, being intellectual and therefore arrogant, criticised people.' In her letters Libussa seems to have been permanently worried about money: after the loss of her husband it was a real struggle to make ends meet. Nevertheless, she was constantly sending money to her son to enable him to live abroad for the sake of his health. Her struggles to make him restrict his expenditure without threatening his real comfort make touching reading. After Melanie married, Libussa continued to worry about her daughter's health, advising her and trying to protect her from the trials of a marriage she feared were too much for her.

Melanie was the youngest of four children, Emilie born in 1876, Emmanuel in 1877, Sidonie in 1878 and Melanie herself on 30 March 1882, shortly after the family moved to Vienna. Family circumstances by the time Melanie was born were somewhat straitened and her mother opened a shop to help keep them. She sold not only plants but also reptiles, which she hated. In her autobiography Klein says that her mother attracted customers by her personality; that many came to her shop to talk rather than to buy. Melanie was handed over to a wet-nurse who fed her on demand, though the older children had all been fed by their mother.

When she grew up Melanie learnt that her arrival had been 'unexpected', though she says she never felt any lack of love. What she does describe is lack of attention, both from her father and, in the beginning, her mother too. She describes a painful memory from the age of 3, of climbing onto her father's lap and being pushed away. Her mother's brother Herman made her a favourite, but this did not really make up for the pain of her father's preference for his older daughter Emilie, and his lack of consideration for Melanie's feelings about this.

When Melanie was 4 and Sidonie 8, Sidonie died after a long illness (scrofula, a form of tuberculosis). Melanie's memory of Sidonie is of her beauty and her kindness. While Emilie and Emmanuel teased her, Sidonie took pity on her little sister and taught her reading and arithmetic. The memories of deep gratitude and affection for her sister remained with Melanie all her life.

> I have a feeling that I never entirely got over the feeling of grief for her death. I also suffered under the grief my mother showed, whereas my father was more controlled. I remember that I felt that my mother needed me all the more now that Sidonie was gone, and it is probable that some of the spoiling was due to my having to replace that child.

Melanie remained convinced to the end of her life that Sidonie would have been a good friend: in her absence, their brother Emmanuel became the closest person to her. From at least the age of 9, when Emmanuel, aged 14, praised and corrected a poem she had written, 'he was my confidant, my friend, my teacher. He took great interest in my development and I knew that, until his death, he always expected me to do something great, although there was really nothing on which to base it.' He taught her Latin and Greek in order to enable her to attend the Gymnasium and encouraged her to have her writing published.

Melanie planned not only to study medicine like her father but to specialise in psychiatry. Her last years at school, under the influence and encouragement of her brother, were years in which she felt 'gloriously alive' (Grosskurth, 1986: 17). She was intellectually and emotionally stimulated by Emmanuel and his friends who discussed Nietzsche, Arthur Schnitzler and Karl Kraus, all radical thinkers who challenged conventional morality. There were at least four friends of her brother's who would have gladly married her.

It seems that Emmanuel and Melanie to some extent united against their older sister and their parents. In one letter to Emmanuel, their mother writes that she is jealous of his confiding in Melanie: she says she never spoilt any of the children by too many demonstrations of affection but he should know he can trust her. Emmanuel too writes to Melanie that he does not always show his affection, and reproaches her for not expressing her affection for him sufficiently. His concern for her and their mother shows through the arrogance and bravado of a young man who knows he is ill and soon to die. Emmanuel's letters are full of admiration and respect for Melanie's beauty as well as for her wisdom and good sense.

Emmanuel was 'rebellious and at times difficult', a factor which Klein attributes to his having been told at 12 that he had a heart condition which would mean he would die young. As his father was also going senile for the last few years of his life, it is not surprising that Emmanuel as the only son found it difficult to behave. This may also have stimulated Melanie to wish to study psychiatry, though some awareness of a depressive reaction of her own to Sidonie's death may also have played a part. Their father died of pneumonia at the age of 72 in April 1900, when Melanie was 18 and Emmanuel 23.

The role of the father does play a part in Klein's work but it is secondary to the role of the mother; in this she provides a very important counter to Freud's view which consistently emphasised the importance of the father. During Klein's childhood it seems her mother ran the household, with her father playing the role of mentor and intellectual standard who was being challenged as his son grew up and his own mind deteriorated.

Her father's deterioration and death may have been at least partly responsible for Melanie agreeing, at the age of 19, to marry Arthur Klein, a chemical engineering student in Zurich. Melanie wrote in her autobiography that she realised very early on that this was a mistake, but was unable to admit it to her mother or her brother: she had never got on well with her older sister who was by now married with troubles of her own. Her mother was suffering at this time from her fears for her son as well as from serious financial worries. Emmanuel was travelling for the sake of his health. The family feared that bad news could be extremely dangerous and Emmanuel was not told about his father's death until two months after the event. Melanie was far more concerned to keep up his spirits than to trouble him with her own problems. Perhaps her mother's model of a dutiful rather than loving wife played a part in her decision to go through with the marriage: certainly Emmanuel and her mother both emphasised the relief to the family finances, and therefore to their mother's worries, of Melanie's proposed marriage.

Emmanuel died in Genoa in December 1902, and Melanie married Arthur the following March. Her marriage was unhappy from the beginning. In her autobiography she wrote 'I threw myself as much as I could into motherhood and interest in my child. I knew all the time that I was not happy but saw no way out.' She did not manage to find any understanding with her husband, and told a student many years later that he was having affairs from the first years of her marriage. For a woman born in 1882 to divorce presented difficulties; she had three children, Melitta born in 1904, Hans in 1907 and Erich in 1914, and no means of supporting them without her husband.

As her own family grew up so 'memories in feeling', as she would later call them (Klein, 1975, III: 181), of the losses of her own childhood must have been evoked. During the years of her marriage Klein was depressed and tense, repeatedly sent on 'cures' for her 'nerves' by her mother and husband, leaving her children in the care of her mother. She attempted to work on her difficulties by writing and she left behind four short stories as well as poetry. In these, she struggles with the issues of sexuality, infidelity, love, friendship, abandonment and death.

All her life, writing seems to have been important for Klein in helping her to overcome the losses she suffered. Her sister had taught her to write shortly before she died, and it was in the pleasures of school that Klein found recovery from this loss. Her link with her father was in intellectual interests; so too her link with her brother Emmanuel. She was always grateful to her husband for his help in finding and publishing her brother's writings after his death. When, later, her son Hans died on a mountain, she turned to writing to help her cope with this loss too. At this time, with the benefits of her own analysis behind her, she wrote one of her most important papers, 'A Contribution to the Psychogenesis of Manic-Depressive States'.

Ferenczi and Psychoanalysis

It was not until she was in her thirties that Klein found any real relief from her depression. She and her family had moved from one small town in Austria-Hungary to another until they settled in 1910 in Budapest. In 1914, the year the war broke out, her third child, Erich, was born and her mother died. Budapest does not seem to have been very much affected by the war at this time, and it was possibly in this year that Klein went into analysis with Sandor Ferenczi, an eminent Hungarian doctor of great charm and intellect, who had embraced and contributed to psychoanalytical ideas. Her analysis with Ferenczi was very important to her, and she seems to have found in analysis a spiritual home. She read Freud's book *On Dreams* and became completely committed to psychoanalysis.

Freud had opened up the study of the unconscious: the part of the mind about which we normally know little yet which deter- mines our actions, feelings and thoughts even more than our con- scious mind. He had found that in this part of the mind were the remnants of infantile thoughts, wishes, and fears about sex, repressed out of consciousness and separated from realisations which would challenge and modify them. These unconscious thoughts and wishes expressed themselves in dreams in a very distorted fashion, symbolised in order to get past the 'censor' in the mind which did not permit such ideas into consciousness. They also expressed themselves, similarly distorted, in 'unintended actions' (such as slips of the tongue) and in neurotic symptoms.

Through his analysis of his own dreams and analysis of others, Freud had also discovered the Oedipus complex. He was less certain about girls' sexual development, but he thought that around the age of 3–5 boys developed a desire to kill their fathers and marry their mothers. This stage lasted for some time, he thought, and when it dissipated the boy was left with a super-ego, the basis of the censor and the conscience, formed from his father's prohibitions against sexual thoughts and desires. There was a feeling among analysts that the repression of such thoughts and feelings could be avoided if children were brought up in a less authoritarian manner. This would protect children against the development of neurotic symptoms later in life and also free their intellect: general intellectual curiosity often underwent repression along with the specific strictures against sexual thoughts.

Freud had observed signs of these processes in adults. He had analysed one small boy through the boy's father, but he had not worked directly with children. He wanted women to become analysts to work with children and to explore the development of female sexuality in greater depth. Klein was one who rose to the challenge.

Klein began to make observations on her own small son, and Ferenczi told her she had a gift for psychoanalytical understanding. Encouraged by this she determined to allow her son's mind freedom from unnecessary prohibitions and distortions of the truth. A freethinker herself, she did not want to teach him that there was a God. She also wanted to be straightforward and truthful with him about sex. This at the time was extremely radical. Her husband, who did believe in God, objected. The results of her efforts are described in a paper she gave to the Budapest Psychoanalytical Society in 1919: called 'The Development of a Child', it was subtitled 'The influence of sexual enlightenment and relaxation of authority on the intellectual development of children'.

In this paper Klein describes the daily development of understanding in her son, aged 5. She shows him learning the meaning of 'I will', 'I must', 'I want to', 'I can'. After several observations on this theme, she describes how he saw a goose and asked whether it could run. 'Just at that moment the goose began to run. He asked, "Is it running because I said it?" On this being denied, he continued, "Because *it* wanted to?"' (Klein, 1975, I: 14). She describes his 'omnipotence feeling' and watches it decline as he learns more about reality.

In attempting to enlighten the child sexually she followed the principle of waiting for his questions and she told him about the egg growing inside the mother. However, he never asked directly about the role of the father. Instead his questions became repetitious and without real interest or meaning. After a time he lost interest in play and eventually 'even showed signs of boredom in his mother's company – a thing that had never occurred before' (Klein, 1975, I: 29). She describes several disturbing changes in the child, including a disinclination to be told stories.

'My growing conviction that repressed sexual curiosity is one of the chief causes for mental changes in children was confirmed by the correctness of a hint I had received a short time previously.' Dr Anton Freund had pointed out that Klein had:

> taken only the conscious and not also the unconscious questions into consideration. At the time I replied that I was of the opinion that it sufficed to deal with conscious questions so long as there was no convincing reason to the contrary. Now however I saw that his view was correct, that to deal only with conscious questions had proved to be insufficient. (Klein, 1975, I: 30)

She accordingly found a way to tell Erich about 'the act of impregnation'. At first he did not want to know, but after she made up a story for him:

> quite spontaneously he began to talk, and from then on he told longer or shorter phantastic stories, originating sometimes in ones he had been told but mostly entirely original and providing a mass of analytic material. Hitherto the child had shown as little tendency to tell stories as to play ... These stories ... produced the effect of dreams from which the secondary elaboration was lacking ... he told them with enormous zest; from time to time as resistances occurred – in spite of careful interpretations – he would interrupt them, only however to resume them again in a short time with enjoyment. (Klein, 1975, I: 31)

She describes in great detail the fantasies Erich related, about horses and cows, soldiers and buildings, in which he makes clear symbolic use of all the objects around him. Erich slipped easily from telling his mother about his fantasies to playing them out and back again to speech. He ran his toys over her body, saying they were climbing mountains; he talked of what babies are made of and said he was making them with his 'poo'; he said he wanted to make babies with his mother. 'He related another phantasy ... in which the womb figured as a completely furnished house, the stomach particularly was very fully equipped and was even possessed of a bath-tub and a soap-dish. He remarked himself about this phantasy, "I know that it isn't really like that, but I see it that way"' (Klein, 1975, I: 35).

As well as telling stories freely, he began to ask questions and to play again: 'He now played gladly and perseveringly, above all with others ... He played at hanging, declared that he had beheaded his brother and sister, boxed the ears of the decapitated heads and said, "One can box the ears of this kind of head, they can't hit back" and called himself a "hanger".' The examples abound. As Klein says:

> His games as well as his phantasies showed an extraordinary

aggressiveness towards his father and also of course his already clearly indicated passion for his mother. At the same time he became talkative, cheerful, could play for hours with other children, and latterly showed such a progressive desire for every branch of knowledge and learning that in a very brief space of time and with very little assistance, he learnt to read.

From appearing somewhat backward, he now appeared 'almost precocious', and his questions lost their stereotyped compulsive character (Klein, 1975, I: 30–1).

During this time Klein went away and left her children for two months. When she came back Erich had developed some fears and phobias which she interpreted. Erich responded enthusiastically.

To begin with, before he starts relating things he enquires quite cheerfully whether what he finds 'horrid' will, after I have explained it, become pleasant again for him just as with the other things so far. He also says that he is not afraid any more of the things that have been explained to him even when he thinks of them. (Klein, 1975, I: 42)

This work with Erich set Klein on the road she was to follow for the rest of her life. Her discovery, for example, that her son could see her as a witch feeding him poison (on her return from being away) may well have prevented her from falling into the trap of believing everything her child patients said about their parents. She learnt at this time how desperately real the child's fantasies were for him, and how much relief could be obtained if the child could be helped to bring these fantasies into contact with thought and reality. Mothers, however bad, are not witches. She recognised that Erich's fear of his mother as a witch stemmed from his own angry wishes towards her, and Erich confirmed this.

She had found evidence for the child's sexual theories which Freud saw as so important. She had watched her son resist sexual enlightenment and become inhibited both intellectually and socially. She had then seen him accept enlightenment with a struggle and had observed the blossoming of his play, intellect and fantasy life which followed and which was accompanied by openly angry and aggressive feelings towards his father and siblings. The benefits to the child of interpreting the symbolism of his play and speech had been demonstrated. It only remained to put this to the test with other children whose creativity was hampered by the repression of sexual thoughts and questions. It was not until Klein reached Berlin that this opportunity arose.

Berlin 1921–1926

In 1919 Melanie Klein was made a member of the Budapest Psychoanalytical Society, but an upsurge of anti-semitism and general political turmoil in Hungary forced her to leave. It was not until five years later that she finally separated from her husband, but this point marked the beginning of the break. Arthur went to Sweden where ultimately he became a Swedish citizen. Melanie took the children to her in-laws in Rosenberg in Slovakia until in 1921 she went to Berlin to continue her psychoanalytical studies. She left her children with the family until she was able to have them join her.

Klein had met the Berlin psychoanalyst Karl Abraham at the International Psycho-Analytic Congress at The Hague in September 1920 and she joined the Berlin Psychoanalytical Society in 1922, the same year that Freud's daughter Anna was made a member of the Vienna Society. Interest in the analysis of children was growing and was developing in several directions. Freud had written up the first analysis of a child, Hans, who had a phobia of horses. Anna Freud was keen to follow in her father's footsteps and she too began analysing children. Her training as a teacher, probably together with Freud's anxieties about the power and risks of the method he had invented, took her in a more didactic direction than Klein, who felt it was important to allow the child freedom from too strict authority and who took pleasure in playing with and listening to children rather than in teaching them. Dr Hug-Hellmuth in Berlin had also begun to analyse children.

Klein by this time had become dissatisfied with the results of her analysis with Ferenczi and asked Abraham to take her into analysis. He agreed and they began in 1924 an analysis which came to an end as a result of Abraham's sudden death in December the following year. She said later that it was her brief analysis with Abraham which really taught her about the practice and theory of analysis. He also supported her when she became worried about the anxiety which emerged when she analysed one of her young patients. He strengthened her resolve to continue interpreting the child's anxiety rather than trying to damp it down in any other way. The results were good and the anxiety did abate with interpretations.

While Abraham was alive Klein found support in Berlin, both personally and in her work with children. However, she was already facing opposition. Fears about the dangers of probing too much in children's unconscious were already surfacing when in 1924 the first analyst to attempt the analysis of children, Hermine

Hug-Hellmuth, was murdered by an 18-year-old nephew she had brought up and attempted to analyse. The boy demanded money from the other analysts for having been used by his aunt as raw material for her work.

Klein had seen too many children significantly helped by analysis to give it up. She defended her own methods of analysis as quite different. Hug-Hellmuth had written that it was necessary to content oneself with 'partial success' and to avoid penetrating too deeply into a child's mind, for fear of stirring up too powerfully the repressed tendencies and impulses or of making demands which their powers of assimilation are unable to meet. She also believed that an analyst should exert an educative influence on a child. Klein disagreed. Arguing that it was impossible to work as a teacher and an analyst at the same time, she said she had found that straightforward analysis of the deepest anxieties of children from 3 to 6 years old was 'both successful and full of promise' (Klein, 1975, I: 139–40).

However, it is notable that in 1925 Klein published the last paper in which she describes the analysis of her own children by herself. (All of these papers disguised the children, but earlier versions of the papers exist.) Her daughter was by now of an age to read her mother's papers and, in addition, removal to London the following year opened up the possibility of finding colleagues she could trust to analyse her children; but Klein must also have been discovering some of the real problems which arise when children are analysed by their parents. She never wrote about this, probably out of respect for Freud's analysis of his daughter Anna, but contented herself with warning her pupils against it. She felt that children needed privacy from their parents, and that the power of the parent in the child's mind should not be increased even further by intrusive attempts to interpret the child's deepest and guiltiest secrets.

The death of Abraham left Klein isolated and friendless in Berlin. It coincided with the ending of a brief but passionate relationship with a journalist nine years younger than herself, and with the departure of Alix Strachey, an Englishwoman also in training as an analyst with Abraham, who had offered some understanding and companionship. Klein was coming under humiliating attack from other analysts, such as Sandor Rado, who knew little of child analysis but were opposed to it. Rado thought all analysts should be doctors and he used his position as editor of the *Internationale Zeitschrift für Psychoanalyse* and Secretary of the Berlin Psychoanalytical Society to prevent Klein's papers being published. Alix Strachey described the atmosphere in the Berlin Society:

Klein gave a paper on the principles of child analysis and at last the opposition showed its hoary head . . . The words used were of course psychoanalytical: danger of weakening the Ich ideal, etc. But the *sense* was I thought purely anti-analysis: We mustn't tell the children the terrible truth about their repressed tendencies etc. And this altho' die Klein demonstrated absolutely clearly that these children (from 2¾ upwards) were already wrecked by the repression of their desires and the most appalling *Schuld Bewusstsein* [sic] [sense of guilt]. (Grosskurth, 1986: 124)

Ernest Jones, the founder of the British Psychoanalytical Society (and later Freud's biographer), had heard a paper given by Klein in 1925 and, encouraged by other English analysts, he invited her to give a series of lectures in England in July of that year. 'The three weeks in which she gave those lectures she considered one of the happiest times of her life' (H. Segal, 1979: 34). Those lectures formed the basis of her book, *The Psychoanalysis of Children*. Instead of the suspicion and rejection of Berlin, she found in England like-minded analysts who valued and respected her work. There was nothing to keep her in Berlin, and nothing to draw her back to her home town. She was already separated from her husband and the future in Europe at this time for a divorced Jewish woman with three children must have seemed bleak.

England 1926

In 1926, at the age of 38, Klein moved to England and became established within the British Psychoanalytical Society. She found there support and friendship, not only from Ernest Jones but also from several other women analysts: Joan Riviere, Susan Isaacs, and later Paula Heimann, all of whom encouraged her and sent her patients. They also helped her both to explain her ideas and convey them in a more comprehensible form.

Klein's practice as a child analyst had begun in Berlin, but in London it expanded. In her book *The Psychoanalysis of Children* she describes her analytical work with small children. The children's fears and beliefs, their play and their fantasies are related in great detail. She conveys to the reader who has some memory of their own childhood a whole new world which has at the same time a sense of familiarity, of 'so *that's* what it's about!' The theoretical chapters in this book are not so readable; Klein was at this time attempting to use a theory which did not fit the observations she was making. She was trying to fit her ideas as closely as possible to Freud's when her observations went further and challenged his.

The years between 1926, when Klein arrived in London, and

1938, when the Freuds arrived and controversies threatened to split the British Psychoanalytical Society, were years of great productivity for Klein. During this time she made many new discoveries about the unconscious life of children. She found that the Oedipus conflict began long before Freud had thought; she observed the complex interplay of guilt and anxiety, love and hatred, and the internal and external worlds in children in a way which was totally new and startling. Freud and Abraham thought that there was a period in which children loved their mothers without conflict: Klein found this was not so and believed that even very small babies had to cope with conflicting feelings of love and hatred. We shall look at some of these ideas in Chapter 2.

In 1930 Klein published 'The Importance of Symbolism in the Development of the Ego' (Klein, 1975, vol. I), describing the analysis of a boy of 4 ('Dick') who showed definite signs of psychosis. This was generally unrecognised in children at this time and her analysis of Dick opened up new investigations. Dick responded to her interpretations in a way he did not respond to people normally, and within a few sessions was beginning to show some attachment to his nurse, where previously he had never shown attachment to anyone. This analysis opened up the possibility of analysing psychotic adults. It drew attention to the plight of many children who suffer from undiagnosed psychoses and was instrumental in the development of the diagnosis of childhood schizophrenia or autism.

Dick gave Klein important clues about the ways a relationship with the mother can go wrong very early on. For example, he took out of the room a truck he had asked Klein to cut up, which Klein understood as showing her how he dealt with his destructiveness by expelling it. His analysis laid the basis for her later understanding of cutting and expelling as the earliest ways of dealing with anxiety in normal development as well as in disturbed children. It also led to the idea of projective identification, which will be taken up in Chapter 2.

One of Klein's colleagues at this time was Susan Isaacs, who founded the Malting House School in Cambridge and later became Principal of the Institute of Education at the University of London. In the Malting House School Isaacs and her staff observed and noted in detail the children's interactions and their intellectual and emotional development. She was able to demonstrate how children had much more ability than adults at the time believed: how their thought and understanding was much more subtle and intelligent, and how their interest could be drawn to the ways things worked in a way which previously would have been considered too advanced for even much older children. She also noted examples of their use of symbolism and interest in sexuality. Isaacs' understanding and careful observations provided backing for many of Klein's ideas and contributed to the development of Kleinian theory.

Mourning and its Relation to Manic-Depressive States

In October 1933 Melitta Schmideberg, Klein's daughter and an analyst herself, began attacking Klein both openly and covertly within the Psychoanalytical Society. Melitta's analyst Edward Glover joined in these attacks: his attachment to Melitta seems to have been more fatherly than professional and he seems to have seen Klein as a rival. Melitta made public accusations against her mother, on one occasion shouting 'Where is the father in your work?', stamping her feet and storming out of the meeting.

Melitta's grievances against her mother were partly focused on the claim that Klein did not pay sufficient attention to external reality in the difficulties of children. However inexcusable Melitta's behaviour, she probably had good reason to be angry with her mother. Melitta must have suffered from the separation of her parents, as well as from her mother's many absences when she was small: at the time the effects of such events were not recognised. Descriptions of the young Melitta in Klein's early papers are also not very complimentary and could well have fuelled Melitta's resentment against her mother. Whatever lay behind them, the attacks became public, embarrassing and virulent, though Klein apparently never retaliated. Melitta and her mother were never reconciled, and at the time of Klein's funeral Melitta was giving a lecture in London.

Six months after these attacks began, in April 1934, Klein's older son Hans was out walking in the Tatra Mountains near his father's relatives where he was staying. The path crumbled beneath him and he fell to his death. Klein was distraught – to the extent that she could not get to the funeral in Budapest. Melitta added to her problems by telling her colleagues that Hans had killed himself, though there was no evidence at all for this, and Klein in fact received a letter from a woman saying that she and Hans had been about to marry.

This death brought back for Klein feelings about the loss of her brother and must have evoked the death of her mother, her father and her sister too. C.Z. Kloetzel, the man she had loved in Berlin, and who, like Hans, resembled her brother Emmanuel, had also left for Palestine in late 1933 and Klein seems to have been in a state of depression from this time.

By the summer Klein had recovered sufficiently to write a paper developing her ideas about depression. Entitled 'A Contribution to the Psychogenesis of Manic-Depressive States' and published in 1935 it 'begins a period of work in which Melanie Klein built a new theoretical structure' (Klein, 1975, I: 432). 'Mourning and its relation to Manic-Depressive States', published five years later, continued the work and described (in a disguised form) from a more bearable distance Klein's own reactions to the death of her son.

In these papers Klein describes what she had begun to call the 'inner world'. She had previously emphasised how babies take their parents into themselves.

> The baby, having incorporated his parents, feels them to be live people inside his body in the concrete way in which deep unconscious phantasies are experienced – they are, in his mind, 'internal' or 'inner' objects . . . Thus an inner world is being built up in the child's unconscious mind, corresponding to his actual experiences and the impressions he gains from people and the external world, and yet altered by his own phantasies and impulses. (Klein, 1975, I: 345)

Klein spells out the way a death causes havoc in the internal world: how the loss of a loved person in the external world leaves the mourner feeling that they have lost a loved mother from their internal world. This leaves them prey to all kinds of bad figures inside. In an attempt to deal with these, manic defences may be used in which the internal world is paralysed or frozen for a time, for example, and all guilt and responsibility for the loss is denied. She describes a dream in which, as Mrs A, she attempted to deny her own loss by making out that it was her mother's son who was to die. She describes her feelings of triumph over her son and her brother who had died, and her triumph over her mother who had lost her son too. Klein describes herself at this time as feeling desperately alone with her loss, vulnerable to a revengeful mother and a revengeful son and brother who had died to punish her. She makes it clear how in this reaction she had lost a sense of her internal mother supporting and loving her, and how long it took to rebuild this. She also describes the limited way in which real people in the external world could help her.

As the reality of the loss is gradually acknowledged, the unreality of the persecutory figures is also recognised. Once Klein admitted her own loss, she no longer triumphed over her mother and brother, and no longer attributed all losses to her mother in an attempt to deny her own. This meant that they were no longer full of revenge towards her but in her mind could share and understand her loss and support her through it. In the discovery of her own jealousy of her brother and her mother, Klein's view of her mother must also have changed and become more realistic. With the increase in the sense of reality and understanding, the good internal mother is regained with a greater sense of wholeness and security.

In these two papers Klein describes repeated magical and illusory attempts to deny the reality of loss. Earlier, in 'Infantile Anxiety-Situations Reflected in a Work of Art and in the Creative Impulse' (Klein, 1975, vol. I), written in 1929, she had described more realistic attempts to restore the inner world by creative work in the external world. Creativity she saw as an attempt to recreate an external and internal world felt to be lost or at risk in a way which did not deny the reality of the loss, of guilt or of responsibility. Her papers are evidence of the reality of her own creative ability to rebuild and renew her internal world as a result of mourning. In her 1935 paper Klein first uses the concept of reparation to describe such work. The 'new theoretical structure' which Klein began to build under the influence of her own grief was real and solid.

Klein connected all of these processes to the task the child faces when at the time of weaning it has to face losses in external reality. She thought that the child at this time too responds with manic defences but gradually gains increased contact with reality in a new way. Her ideas about the depressive position, formulated in these papers, continued to develop.

The Arrival of the Freuds

As the Nazis came to power in Austria many Jewish analysts were forced to leave Vienna. The controversies about the different approaches to children and to child analysis were sharpened by the arrival in London of both Sigmund and Anna Freud (who came in 1938) and other colleagues from Vienna. By this time Klein had been in England for twelve years and had established herself as a leading theoretician and training analyst. She soon found herself and her work under attack. Her distress was made worse by her conviction that her own way of working was closer to Freud's than his daughter's was.

Tensions within the British Psychoanalytical Society rose during the early years of the war. Many factors were probably involved. Many disagreements became personalised by Klein's daughter Melitta and Edward Glover in a very unpleasant way. In addition, considerations of power, status and competitiveness were heightened by the economic difficulties of the war and the influx of analysts chasing too few patients. There were also general feelings aroused by the implicit claim of Freud's daughter to be the standard bearer for psychoanalysis in a Psychoanalytical Society which had been developing its own work in relative freedom and in the firm belief that it was working along lines Freud would eventually approve. In addition, the fact that the 'enemy aliens', which included Anna Freud and the other Viennese analysts, were not allowed to leave London during the bombing, while other analysts could and did, also gave rise to bad feeling. There may well also have been quite unmentionable undercurrents of feeling to do with British anti-semitism as well as British and Austrian nationalism, and the need for analysts to counteract both within themselves.

The Controversial Discussions

From 1942 to 1943 a series of discussions, later called the Controversial Discussions, were set up to sort out the differences between the followers of Klein and the followers of Anna Freud. These were kept private to the British Society until 1986 when they were described by Phyllis Grosskurth in her biography of Klein. She traces some of the complex political issues involved, as well as some of the substance of the arguments. In 1990 these discussions, with the addition of relevant letters, were eventually published as a book, *The Freud–Klein Controversies 1941–45* (King and Steiner, 1990). Many of the issues raised are still live topics for disagreement today and they are taken up in Chapter 4.

The discussions began with Susan Isaacs' paper, 'The Nature and Function of Phantasy' (Klein et al., 1952), and eventually this paper and the discussion it aroused took up four meetings of the Society between January and April 1943. One of the questions on the agenda was whether Klein's work was psychoanalysis or whether it was to be thrown out as Rank's, Adler's, Reich's and Jung's had been. Control of subcommittees and functions (such as training, research and publications) was a serious consideration, with the potential for destroying Klein's work and her ability to teach students. At one point Anna Freud resigned from the Society over the issue of training.

Eventually the Society managed to work out a compromise whereby Anna Freud and her co-workers, and Klein and hers, could both train their own students. A further group of analysts, called the 'Middle Group', consisted of those who did not want to admit allegiance to either. This system continues today, though the 'Middle Group' are now known as the 'Independents'.

Klein was very distressed by these discussions. Her failure to convince Freud of her views had been a great disappointment to her, and the lengths to which analysts such as Glover were prepared to go to discredit her were extremely upsetting. On the other hand, she was supported not only by Joan Riviere, Susan Isaacs and Paula Heimann but also by many other British analysts, such as W.R.D. Fairbairn, who went along with her ideas to a greater or lesser extent.

Ernest Jones stayed out of the way in his country house, pleading illness: this too must have been a disappointment, though Klein wrote to Susan Isaacs (Grosskurth, 1986: 309) that she had not expected better; she knew he was too weak to be able to cope with supporting her against Anna Freud. It would not have been surprising if Jones had really been ill: he had wanted to marry Anna Freud when he was younger, but it was he who had invited Klein to England and had repeatedly backed her publicly and privately. He had even sent his own children to her for analysis. (His placatory letters to both Klein and Anna Freud, published in *The Freud–Klein Controversies*, make amusing reading.) By staying out of the way he left the conduct of the meetings to Glover. To what extent the difficulties of the male medical analysts, such as Jones and Glover, were increased by the fact that the work under discussion was that of extremely intelligent and competent non-medical women it is difficult to know. Glover, writing to Jones (Grosskurth, 1986: 343) about the difficulties, commented that they agreed 'it was a woman ridden Society (your favoured hypothesis)'. Many of the more able men were on active service and unable to attend the meetings. The most original and perceptive contributions to both sides of the discussion came from women, most of them without medical degrees.

During this time Klein and Anna Freud, as well as the other analysts involved, were all working out their own ideas. The discussions forced them to sort out some very tricky areas of disagreement, and to recognise some of the areas where insufficient knowledge was available.

New Developments 1946–1957

In 1946 Klein published one of her most important papers, 'Notes on Some Schizoid Mechanisms', dealing with precisely the issues which had been under most discussion: the mental functioning of an infant in the first 3 months and its relation with the mother. A further stimulus to this paper was the fact that Fairbairn had published a paper on the origins of schizophrenia in which views very close to Klein's were expressed. Fairbairn, working on his own in Edinburgh, was less perturbed than Klein that his ideas were incompatible with some of Freud's.

In this paper Klein discusses some of the mechanisms which underlie both many ordinary aspects of life and also schizophrenia. This paper began a new era for Klein. From this time on her papers acknowledge her debt to Freud but also her disagreements with him. She takes hold of her material and develops her ideas and theories to fit the observations she has made. The challenge from her opponents combined with the support and intellectual rigour of her close colleagues to stimulate the development of radical theories which were expressed in a much clearer and more powerful manner.

In May 1947 Klein published a postscript to her paper 'Symposium on Child Analysis' in which she describes in detail the changes Anna Freud had made to her technique of child analysis according to a book *The Psycho-analytical Treatment of Children*, published in 1946. These changes brought Anna Freud's technique and ideas much closer to Klein's. However, Anna Freud makes no acknowledgement of Klein and this, together with opposition from other analysts, contributed to Klein's fears that her work would not survive.

Students and Schizophrenia

After the war, Klein's work with psychotic processes was developed not only by herself but also by several very gifted students whom she inspired, supported and encouraged, though as far as we know she never supervised any of them in their work with psychoses. W.C.M. Scott, Herbert Rosenfeld and Hanna Segal were able to analyse people suffering from schizophrenia. Previously, analysts had claimed that this was impossible and had either avoided taking on people who were severely disturbed or had, like Anna Freud with children, backed off from analysing the anxieties they met. Some had responded with reassurance or other attempts to 'gain the confidence' of the patient, which Klein pointed out prevented the development of an analytical relationship. With Klein's encouragement and belief in the analytic process, her pupils simply analysed their patients in spite of the anxiety this aroused in them. This work was taken further not only by Segal and Rosenfeld but also by Wilfred Bion, who went into analysis with Klein after the war and became a member of the Psychoanalytical Society in 1950.

Paula Heimann was a colleague and analysand of Klein's who became a close friend and also took further some of Klein's insights. Her support and writing at the time of the Controversial Discussions had been important. In 1950 Heimann wrote a very influential paper 'On Countertransference'. Counter-transference refers to the feelings arising in an analyst in response to a patient and has been the subject of continuous debate from the beginning of psychoanalysis. Klein disagreed with the thesis of this paper: she felt that the analyst's feelings for the patient should simply be considered as a disturbance of the analyst's and not as a communication between patient and analyst. Yet it was her insights which permitted this interpretation of the analyst's feelings. Like Freud, she seems to have become somewhat nervous as her pupils took up her ideas with fervour; and she reacted as if they were throwing all caution and common sense to the wind. However, the idea of the patient projecting aspects of themselves into the analyst in a way that the analyst could detect them was such a powerful one that it could not be ignored. Not only Rosenfeld and Segal but Bion in particular worked with this idea.

Klein's relation with Heimann developed from friendship, to analyst-patient and collaborator. However, in 1957 Heimann broke with Klein, objecting strongly to Klein's ideas about envy, though personal issues seem to have been involved too.

New Directions in Psychoanalysis

By the time Klein was 70 in 1952, she had achieved some limited measure of respectability within the psychoanalytical community. Her opponents did not read her papers or attend meetings at which Kleinian ideas were to be discussed, but a birthday issue of *The International Journal of Psycho-Analysis*, edited by Heimann and Money-Kyrle, was devoted to papers by eleven of her pupils and colleagues. In 1955 most of these, plus two papers by herself, were published in a book entitled *New Directions in Psychoanalysis*. This is a thoroughly readable book. A 'clinical' section contains descriptions of work with patients and clear and perceptive statements of new Kleinian ideas on schizophrenia, schizoid mechanisms, speech and symbol formation. Papers in the 'applied' section use Klein's ideas to add new insight in the fields of aesthetics, art, literature and ethics.

Envy and Gratitude

At around this time Klein began a new and final dramatic contribution to psychoanalytical theory which was published in her book *Envy and Gratitude*. According to Hanna Segal, she became very depressed during the time she was writing this book. The loss of Heimann's friendship and affection must have contributed, reviving the many other losses in her life, including her loss of hope for recognition from Freud himself or even Anna Freud. Klein was worried about the future of psychoanalysis in particular and the world in general. The threat of nuclear war was also a worry for her. Hanna Segal (1979: 151) says that the threat of Klein's own approaching death may have contributed to her fears for the survival of her work.

Envy and Gratitude is a book which is readable and comprehensible to the general reader as well as to the analyst. In it Klein spells out in great detail the way in which a small baby can attack its mother's breast out of envy. It is not only bad behaviour or frustration or pain which causes the baby to attack the breast, but sometimes the experience of a good feed. She goes on to describe vividly some of the manifestations of envy in adult life. She maintains that one of the roots of penis envy is displaced envy of the breast, thereby challenging one of the bastions of male superiority: it is *women's* possessions and attributes which are originally more valued and therefore envied than men's.

The concept of envy draws attention to the way in which disturbance can arise in the presence of good mothering. A bad feeding experience may give rise to a sense that the breast has unlimited food and love which it is keeping for itself; a good experience can for some babies (and adults) be intolerable because it heightens awareness of the baby's own lack. The baby attacks the breast felt to be good, giving and creative: in later life this appears as denigration of mothers; as mockery of people felt to have more than the self; as an inability to keep in mind the goodness of something seen as not belonging to the self. This process is extremely damaging, preventing the baby (and later the adult) from enjoying life since enjoyment itself is under attack.

Klein made it very clear that the good internal breast, seen as the source of love and goodness inside, is also under attack by envy. If this attack is successful the person no longer has a centre of goodness inside them. Other people who seem to have this centre may be envied: if they in turn are successfully attacked and spoiled, then there is no hope for the self ever to gain peace. Such people live in a world of complaint and misery surrounded by unhappiness inside themselves and outside.

It is clear from this book that Klein was seeking an explanation as to why it was that however good her interpretations were *and were felt to be* they could be greeted with negative reactions. After a session in which a patient felt helped, they could come back devaluing and complaining about the analyst and analysis. This was repeated again and again.

She also describes the shock and happiness which can follow the interpretation of envious destructiveness. A woman patient was brought to see through a dream that it was owing to her envy that she felt suspicious of the analyst, convinced that the analyst was feeding herself and other people, not the patient:

> The response to the analysis of the dream was a striking change in the emotional situation. The patient now experienced a feeling of happiness and gratitude more vividly than in previous analytic sessions. She had tears in her eyes, which was unusual, and said that she felt as if she now had had an entirely satisfactory feed. It also occurred to her that her breast-feeding and her infancy might have been happier than she had assumed. Also, she felt more hopeful about the future and the result of her analysis. (Klein, 1975, III: 205–6)

Klein is clear that she had known she was envious and jealous of other people but she had not seen how much she was spoiling the analysis with her envy. Interpretation of envy allows the possibility of recognising real goodness and value in the outside world without destroying it. As envy can spoil and destroy everything of value, both outside and ultimately inside the self, so the discovery and interpretation of it can enrich and improve life enormously.

Klein gives us a very powerful and complex understanding of envy and the defences against it (which may be indistinguishable from it). Her book makes sense of many of the difficulties of everyday life, particularly in any situation where there is a giver and recipient or any kind of inequality. For a counsellor or therapist it is essential reading.

The ideas published in *Envy and Gratitude* in 1957 once again created a furore. Winnicott apparently sat throughout the presentation of the original paper with his head in his hands murmuring 'Oh no, she *can't* do this' (Grosskurth, 1986: 414). Paula Heimann broke with her at this point.

The idea that a newborn baby could feel at all had been a stumbling block for many analysts. Others were happy with the idea that the baby could experience love towards the breast/mother but they balked at the idea of the baby hating the breast. Others found it tolerable that the baby could love and hate the breast/mother as long as the hatred was seen as a response to some kind of failure on the part of the breast/mother. The idea of envy of the penis had achieved respectability over the years. But the idea that the baby could hate and try to destroy a breast/mother felt to be good, loving and feeding was a step which turned more analysts against Klein. For others, this idea was, like the rest of Klein's work, a shock to the system but one which made sense and which opened up possibilities for understanding which had not existed in the analytical world before.

This work was also important for an understanding of groups, in particular throwing light on the question of why it is so difficult for a group to tolerate new ideas and creative thinking.

Recapitulation: *The Narrative of a Child Analysis*

In her autobiographical notes Klein says that her pessimistic mood accompanying the writing of *Envy and Gratitude* did not last. Gradually her confidence in the future returned: she was encouraged by her pupils' creative work. She took pleasure in the support of friends, colleagues and students. She was also very happy in her relationship with her growing grandchildren, particularly Michael, the eldest. 'As he expressed it later, she had become for him more than just the good granny of his childhood. He had reached an age at which he could appreciate her greatness and feel privileged in having a close relationship with her' (H. Segal, 1985: 151–2).

During the last four years of her life Klein did not add more to her theory. She reduced her work load and took time to produce a final book, *Narrative of a Child Analysis* (Klein, 1975, vol. IV). This was a detailed day-by-day description of an analysis of a boy she called Richard, aged 10, which she had undertaken in Pitlochry in Scotland during the war. It was not ideal; she and Richard knew it was limited to four months; the town was small, they met and he heard about her more than she would have liked; and the room she used was not the best. However, she had taken careful notes and there were few enough sessions to make a manageable book. She included a series of notes after each session which described how she would have seen the material later and pointed out some of her own mistakes. Chapter 3 contains extracts from this book.

Towards the end of her life Klein travelled and had a busy social life. She enjoyed the theatre, music and good company. However, she was also lonely and, characteristically, she determined to write a paper on the topic. In this paper she refers:

> not to the objective situation of being deprived of external companion-ship. I am referring to the inner sense of loneliness – the sense of being alone regardless of external circumstances, of feeling lonely even when among friends or receiving love. This state of internal loneliness, I will suggest, is the result of a ubiquitous yearning for an unattainable perfect internal state.
>
> Such loneliness, which is experienced to some extent by everyone, springs from paranoid and depressive anxieties which are derivatives of the infant's psychotic anxieties. These anxieties exist in some measure in every individual but are excessively strong in illness; therefore loneliness is also part of illness, both of a schizophrenic and depressive nature. (Klein, 1975, III: 300)

This recognition of the loneliness of the psychotic state is typical of Klein's sympathy for people who are deeply disturbed. While she recognised cruelty and attacks, she also recognised the distress which people suffered as a result of these. As she interpreted Richard's attacks, she conveyed her sympathy for his guilt and anxiety about them and her understanding of why he felt he had to do these terrible things. One of her earliest papers had described how criminal acts can arise out of an unconscious sense of guilt ('Criminal Tendencies in Normal Children' (1927): Klein, 1975, vol. I); the idea that a person suffering from schizophrenia might be extremely lonely is equally startling and important. She points out how hard it is to detect the pain and suffering of schizophrenia since the person uses withdrawal and distraction as defences against them. She goes on to say that she is optimistic about the therapeutic outcome of analysis with such people: 'there is an urge towards integration, even in such ill people, and . . . there is a relation however undeveloped, to the good object and the good self.'

In 1958 a discussion with Klein and a group of sympathetic analysts was recorded (Grosskurth, 1986: 442). She spoke on many topics. She said she had never found that counter-transference helped the patient, only the analyst: there was a saying in Berlin: 'If you feel like that about your patient, go in a corner and think it out carefully: what is wrong with *you*?' But she thought it was vital to put yourself in the patient's shoes. She said one cannot always cure everybody, though one can help a great number of people. She felt Freud was too much interested in the scientific aspects of psychoanalysis and not sufficiently concerned for his patients.

Talking about the number of sessions, she was adamant that five times a week was essential. If the patient could not afford it the analyst should reduce his or her fees. Pressed, she said that anything less would be psychotherapy and she could not do it. Here she was making a point to analysts who wanted to reduce the number of hours when she could see no good reason for it: in fact she had seen some patients during the war on an irregular basis and she had seen Paula Heimann briefly less than five times a week. This, perhaps, was experience which made her discourage her students from it.

1960

Towards the middle of 1960 Klein began to feel very exhausted and unwell. This was misdiagnosed as being the natural consequence of age and hard work and she went on holiday to

Switzerland where she met up with Mrs Esther Bick, a pupil and friend. Eventually she had a severe haemorrhage and returned to London, where an operable cancer was diagnosed. She was relieved to be in hospital and was feeling hopeful though also apprehensive. She was keen to finish the *Narrative of a Child Analysis* and was able to revise the proofs while in hospital. She made preparations for her death, leaving instructions with colleagues about her supervisees and remaining patients and discussing the policy for future publications. The Melanie Klein Trust had been set up in 1955 to further psychoanalytical research and teaching: the copyright of her books was given to this trust. She also discussed her funeral arrangements, insisting that no religious service of any description should be part of them.

The operation was successful and the doctors, family, friends and Klein herself felt very optimistic. However, a few days later she fell out of bed and broke her hip, developed complications and died. Hanna Segal says 'Despite her age and the gravity of her illness, this death produced surprise and shock. She had been so active and creative up to the last moment, so present and well in touch with her friends, her family and the psychoanalytical community, that her death was felt as unexpected and untimely' (H. Segal, 1979: 160).

Hanna Segal in her book *Klein* (1979) says that Klein saw herself as the principal successor of Freud and Abraham and her ambitions were ambitions for psychoanalysis rather than for herself; it seems, though, that she did at times confuse the two. Segal writes:

> Although she was tolerant, and could accept with an open mind the criticisms of her friends and ex-pupils, whom she often consulted, this was so only so long as one accepted the fundamental tenets of her work. If she felt this to be under attack she could be very fierce in its defence. And if she did not get sufficient support from those she considered her friends, she could grow very bitter, sometimes in an unjust way. (H. Segal, 1979: 170)

According to Segal, Klein was unjust to both Freud and Jones when they failed to support her entirely, even though she knew that both were pulled by loyalty to Anna. However, when Jones died Klein corrected an obituary written by Winnicott, asking him to insert more about Jones' kindness and helpfulness. She wrote:

> I think the counterpart of Jones's at times sharp and caustic attitude needs much more stressing, that is the great deal of kindness, which expressed itself in helping so many people, and which had its root in a dislike of falsity and mediocrity, and in a real enthusiasm for the value of psychoanalysis. He hated to see it badly or not genuinely represented. (Grosskurth, 1986: 441)

Klein was also noted for being caustic. Her view was 'there could be no compromise in scientific matters . . . One cannot pretend that things can be "a bit like this and a bit like that" in order to appease or placate an opponent.' Hanna Segal writes:

At an international congress a psychoanalyst spoke at great length about the dangers of the analyst falling in with the patient's idealisation of her. Mrs Klein replied saying that if Dr X took a bit more trouble in understanding the paranoid anxieties and the negative transference underlying such an idealisation of herself, she would not feel so much at risk of self-idealisation. On another occasion in the British Society there was a discussion in which it was argued that the analyst must not aim at being perfect – that it was good for the patient to discover the failings of the analyst and that the mistakes of the analyst promoted the development of the patient. Mrs Klein said that her colleagues must feel very near perfection if they thought their failings and mistakes were such a matter for self-congratulation. As for herself, she found that even if she tried her best, she made quite enough mistakes as it was; and when accused of perfectionism she said it was not a matter of not making mistakes – everybody makes mistakes – but of recognising mistakes for what they were and trying to correct them, the important thing being not to elevate mistakes into theories. (H. Segal, 1979: 172)

Jean MacGibbon became friendly with Klein in the last year of her life as a result of writing an article about her work. She invited her to the theatre and to parties which she thoroughly enjoyed. Segal says she also very much enjoyed sitting 'listening' to babies: Grosskurth says that her grandchildren remember her as always ready to listen to them. Ilse Hellman, a leading member of Anna Freud's group, recalled what 'a lovely way she had with children. She was like a jolly, nice granny' who told stories and played with them. Michael Clyne, her grandson, was on holiday with her when she observed a child at the next table misbehaving. 'Klein's expression of sorrowing empathy as she watched him remained with Michael for the rest of his life' (Grosskurth, 1986: 437).

At the unveiling of the plaque to Melanie Klein in St John's Wood, London, Hanna Segal spoke movingly of Klein and the house in which she lived.

Apart from seeing her patients and supervisions Mrs Klein held through the years a regular postgraduate seminar. There she shared her discoveries, discussed her ideas and we were inspired by the freshness of her new approach. As a teacher she was generous, inspiring and never stifling. She stimulated creativity of others and was ungrudging in her help and comments. She was always respectful and encouraging to our own ideas.

I like to think of this house as a cradle of new generations of analysts and new ideas.

She was a rich personality with many facets. But what stands out in my memory is her warm generosity, her spontaneity, sometimes to the point of impetuosity. She had a gift for intimacy and contact and a total lack of pretensions. I like to think of it as a gift for equality. Though one could not forget her stature and she herself was aware of it, particularly in her later years, her relationship with her friends was experienced by both parties as one of equals.

2

Klein's Major Theoretical Contributions

Klein's theoretical contributions were based on the work of Freud but went further and challenged many of his ideas. Joan Riviere, Susan Isaacs, Paula Heimann, Wilfred Bion, Herbert Rosenfeld and Hanna Segal all contributed aspects of what is today considered to be 'Kleinian theory'.

The next chapter (Chapter 3) gives detailed discussion of Klein's case material. As Klein's theories depend very closely on the observations she made in the consulting room, many of her ideas are difficult to believe without a description of the behaviour and words of the children she saw. Some readers will therefore find the present chapter easier to comprehend when they have read Chapter 3.

Klein's theoretical formulations are complex and interwoven. Her own writings explain her ideas, and the evidence for them, in four volumes; one chapter here cannot describe all of her contributions to psychoanalytical theory. I have therefore selected some of the more striking ideas and tried to make them comprehensible to a general reader. Others may be found in the works listed in a Kleinian Reading List at the end of this book.

'Phantasy'

Klein had a quite distinctive view of the inner world, the world of fantasy, and its relation with the external world. Listening to her son Erich at the ages of 4 and 5, with the insights of Freud's work on dreams, Klein found that he saw his mother and the other people around him through 'phantasies' which were constructed from external reality modified by his own feelings and existing beliefs and knowledge. His perception of his mother was clearly influenced by his own emotional state. When he was feeling angry with her, he saw her as a witch threatening to poison him. When he was feeling happy and loving towards her, he saw her as a princess he wanted to marry.

As she extended her work it gradually became clear to her that children relate to the whole world through their unconscious fantasies. Nothing is seen simply as it is: some kind of unconscious fantasy is attached to every perception: structuring, colouring and adding significance to it. Following Strachey, Klein used the word 'phantasy' for unconscious fantasies to distinguish them from conscious fantasies.

Freud had mentioned how parents were seen through the filter of the child's own emotional state and had implied in passing that this could contribute to the child's super-ego: the conscience which forbade certain 'bad' behaviours. However, his writing emphasised the behaviour of the adults around; for example, actually threatening to 'cut off your willy' giving rise to boys' fears of castration. It was such threats, he thought, which made children repress their 'naughty' thoughts.

Klein thought that parents' real behaviour was important; but she became convinced that repression of the child's sexual feelings or thoughts was likely to be caused as much by the child's own sense of guilt or anxiety as by any actual threats from the parents. It was the boy's unconscious jealous, angry or envious impulses to cut off his father's 'willy', for example, which were most important in determining his fears of being castrated himself. It was the girl's angry, jealous or envious desires to take over, spoil and destroy the contents of her mother's breast and body which led to her fear of her mother doing the same to her.

She found too that a fear that *thinking something can make it happen* contributed to the child's anxieties about sexual fantasies and to the child's motivation to hide them. One of the ways of dealing with such terrifying fear was to attribute it to a parent-figure. Instead of thinking 'I mustn't think those thoughts' the child was convinced that the parent was saying '*Do not* think those thoughts.'

Freud's ideas were turned upside down. Rather than the parents creating guilt about sexual thoughts in children who otherwise would not fear them, Klein thought this guilt could arise from the child's own phantasies, in which the child attributed to parents thoughts which did not necessarily belong to them at all.

Klein thought that the importance of parents' actual behaviour lay in the way it was taken by the child as confirmation or disproof of existing phantasies. Parents added new elements to children's phantasy world but generally these tended to reduce the terrifying aspect of the child's phantasies: however well or badly parents behaved reality was less monstrous than the child's phantasies.

The story of Cinderella can be used to illustrate some of Klein's ideas. If we consider how a real girl would feel if her mother died, we can imagine how she might long for her mother to come back. A step-mother might be greeted with very mixed feelings; on the one hand, the child wants a mother-figure who will magically make everything better; on the other, she fears a destructive and scheming woman who will be envious of her beauty and jealous of her relationship with her father. These characteristics are ones we might expect a step-daughter to sense in herself: a hope for magical abilities to make everything right again and fears of her own envy and jealousy towards her father's new wife.

Cinderella's fairy-godmother and step-mother could represent two different phantasies of a real step-mother combined with characteristics of a real step-daughter. In reality, no step-mother can be either a fairy-godmother or as bad and horrible as Cinderella's step-mother.

Klein thought that destructive behaviour by adults left damaging phantasies which would have a long-term effect, but even here it was important to help the child to disentangle reality from the child's own interpretation of events. A real-life Cinderella might well have to cope with real ill treatment: she would be more able to deal with it if she could distinguish her step-mother's actual motives from Cinderella's own feelings towards her.

In Chapter 3 we shall quote from sessions with Richard, aged 10, described by Klein in her *Narrative of a Child Analysis*. Richard showed Klein in great detail how in phantasy he often attacked and damaged his father out of jealous rivalry. Much of this was totally unconscious: he seldom allowed himself to know how much he hated and feared his father. Richard was extremely distressed when his father fell down and became ill in reality; he understood this as confirmation of his fear that his aggressive feelings towards his father could cause real damage. His difficulties quite clearly arose more from the meaning he attached to this event from his own inner world of phantasy than from the event itself.

Richard did not think in terms of the words 'jealous rivalry': his experience was of very strong feelings which led him to 'operate on' a moth which for him symbolised his father: phantasies give 'body' and expression to emotional states.

Klein used the concept of phantasy to describe the active and 'concrete' nature of, for example, mechanisms of defence, as well as the results of these mechanisms. Repression of a dangerous impulse, for example, may be represented in phantasy as chopping up something frightening and pushing it down a hole, or putting it into a can with a lid on: the repressed impulse may be then feared as 'worms' waiting to jump out and wreak havoc. The defence of identification with the aggressor might involve a phantasy of actually taking the aggressor inside the self in an attempt to control them, then feeling controlled by them and needing to get rid of other, threatened and more vulnerable parts of the self into someone else (the new victim).

It may be clear why Klein felt that 'object relations' were so important: phantasies are about doing something to someone, an object distinct from the self. This 'object' could be a part of the self separated off and objectified, that is, seen as 'not me'. Impulses are always experienced, Klein thought, as embodied in some phantasy.

Klein, then, saw the perceptions of infants, children and even adults as actively influenced by their emotional state. Out of the interaction between their emotions and their perception of the world around them and inside them they create phantasies which they use to understand the world. In these phantasies, people and parts of people live and die inside and outside the self; move around; give rise to enormous gratification and equally enormous fear, jealousy, or envy; are pushed from one person to another, either regardless of behaviour or in accordance with subtle or less subtle behaviour. Reality-testing involves examining the results of such phantasy operations on others as well as discovering the limits of the effectiveness of such phantasies. In this way phantasies strongly influence expectations and interpretations of real events in the world.

Many phantasies seem totally real: others have attached to them an awareness that things are not really like this. Klein's son Erich said 'I know it isn't really like that, but I see it like that'; at other times he did not know it 'wasn't really like that', either because he was too young to know (that he could not make babies out of 'poo', for example) or because he did not want to know (that he had been so angry with his mother while she was away that he had wished she was dead, for example).

Phantasies of Attack

Many of the theoretical constructions we shall be describing involve phantasies of attacks on the mother or parts of her body. The idea that babies and small children could want to hurt and damage their mothers, even before they see her as a whole person, is one which many people find difficult to believe. However, it is crucial to an understanding of Klein's work.

Suckling itself involves a biting movement: hitting the breast can also make the milk flow. Klein found that the earliest relation with the mother involved phantasied attacks of many kinds upon her breast. Parents who have walked up and down with screaming babies who will not be comforted may have observed them arching away from a proffered breast or bottle, hitting it and throwing themselves about in a way which certainly could be interpreted as an attempt to destroy everything, including the (sometimes desperate) parent. What is successfully attacked in these situations is the babies' perception: a screaming baby cannot see or hear clearly, and physical feelings are changed by the screaming. It makes sense to wonder if the baby's perception in some primitive way is that the world itself and everything in it has been destroyed by the screaming.

Klein observed her patient Dick at 4 years old terrified of his own aggressiveness and quite unable to defend himself even when he fell over. She linked this with his severe difficulties in eating and making relationships with people, including his mother and his nurse. Fear of his own sadism meant that he believed he could not come close to them and take from them without damaging them irreparably. A child who is too frightened of his own sadism, of his desire to attack and ability to damage the breast or the mother, may be unable to eat or to relate to the mother at all. Much of Klein's work examines the relationship between aggressive and loving impulses and phantasies.

If we look at the Cinderella story again, as written for ordinary little girls who envy their live mothers, we may see how it illustrates various different forms of attack on a mother and her functions. The only good mother in the story is a dead one: the live mother is not Cinderella's beautiful mother at all but is ugly herself and has produced two ugly monsters: her husband is absent and preferred his previous wife (and Cinderella herself). The fairy-godmother, like the coach and horses she creates, is good and has her own magic wand, but the price she pays is that she only exists for Cinderella and has no other life at all, certainly no sexual partner.

At the end of the story Cinderella openly gets her revenge on her sisters and her mother either by punishing them or by being magnanimous and better than them: the story itself has satisfied, perhaps, an ordinary little girl's desires for revenge on a sexual mother preferred by her father, with a life and daughters of her own.

This is the kind of ordinary hidden attack on parents which Klein observed in the material children brought to her. Many of the children were disturbed, but others were brought by parents 'for prophylactic reasons', to prevent possible future neuroses.

The Concept of Positions

Klein found that Freud's concept of stages of development through which a child passes in well-defined order was too limiting. Like Freud, she did think that children's primary interest shifted from oral, to anal and then genital concerns, but she found that there was constant movement from one to the other and back again. She also found that there were certain constellations of attitudes and mechanisms which worked together, acting upon these preoccupations. She described the *paranoid-schizoid position* and the *depressive position* as different ways of dealing with anxiety.

Klein's idea of 'positions' differed from Freud's 'stages' in that she did not think we grow out of them. She felt that there was a continuous tension between paranoid-schizoid mechanisms and depressive mechanisms. People constantly move from one to the other and back again. Throughout life the paranoid-schizoid mechanisms and phantasies are available and are likely to be used when under any kind of stress.

The Paranoid-Schizoid Position

In the earliest period of life, under the influence of frightening phantasies of annihilation in which life itself is under threat, good and bad need to be kept apart. It is important at this stage to distinguish between good and bad, and the danger comes from a muddling of the two.

For example, a phantasy of a nipple which is loving, feeding, creative and good at first needs to be kept quite distinct from phantasies of a nipple which is biting, hurtful and terrifying. Without this splitting the baby may not be able to distinguish fully between love and cruelty and to feed trustingly. Later, adults may continue this separation, keeping apart quite different pictures of their parents and people in general. A father or mother may be seen on the one hand as a weak, kind, loving person and on the other as powerful, undermining and dangerous. The two perceptions may never be recognised as relating to the same person. Where this process has failed, any expression of love may have concealed within it some form of cruelty. Child abuse seems to involve this confusion between love and cruelty.

Klein understood that the processes of splitting the object into bad and good, ideal and terrifyingly persecuting, itself became a threat after a time. It is important to distinguish between good and bad, but deeply splitting a mother or father into a fairy-godmother and a wicked step-mother is a distortion of reality. Splitting is an action undertaken in phantasy which can be used to separate things which belong together.

A 2-year-old resisting weaning said with a delightful smile: 'I wish you were dead mummy then I could cut off your breast and have it all to myself.' In his phantasy he was splitting his mother into a giving breast and a withholding mother: the act of doing so is quite clearly understood as a cut. He was, however, denying the aggressiveness of both his death-wishes and his cutting impulse with the smile.

When one set of perceptions and phantasies is kept apart from another, the child splits not only the object but also him or herself. The good infant loving the good mother/breast and the bad infant hating the bad mother/breast may in the baby's perception be quite different people. Adults often have perceptions of themselves as more than one self. They might say 'I'm not feeling myself today' or 'That wasn't like me' when they have done something which surprised them. The child who hates his or her brother is a child full of hate and capable of attacking in anger; the same child loving his or her brother is a child full of love who may at times forget or deny that he or she ever wanted to destroy this brother. Erna, aged 6, played that:

> a teacher and a mistress – represented by a toy man and woman – were giving the children lessons in manners, teaching them how to bow and curtsy etc. At first the children were good and polite (just as Erna herself always did her best to be good and behave nicely), then suddenly they attacked the teacher and mistress, trampled them underfoot and killed and roasted them. They now became devils, and gloated over the torments of their victims. But all at once the teacher and mistress were in heaven and the former devils had turned into angels, who, according to Erna's account, knew nothing about ever having been devils – indeed 'they never *were* devils'. God the father, the former teacher, began kissing and embracing the woman passionately, the angels worshipped them and all was well again – though before long the balance was sure to be disturbed again one way or another. ((Klein, 1975, II: 37).

In this example, Erna is seeing the teacher and the mistress as embodying aspects of her own cruelty and her own reparative impulses: her mother was not in fact as cruel and destructive as she often fantasised and Erna recognised this later in her analysis. The process of sorting out good and bad objects involves projection of parts of the self. Splitting thus creates larger-than-life people and larger-than-life emotions, unmodified by their opposites. Perception is distorted so that, for example, if someone or something is defined as bad, any goodness in them is simply not seen. Where splitting is less severe, such goodness may be seen but attributed to someone else, as in: 'I know my father is nice sometimes, but it's only when my mother makes him.' Denial functions on many levels.

Phantasies in which parts of others are taken into the self (introjection) are also extremely important. Where this takes place under the influence of the paranoid-schizoid position the parts taken in will be split and idealised: larger-than-life and wonderful or excessively persecuting and dangerous. The boundary between self and other is in some ways denied, and the self may be felt to be attached to or identical with a very powerful idealised other who can do no wrong. This idealisation covers a conviction that this other is really frightening and aggressive, diminishing the self, humiliating and destructive. This may be the basis of a kind of arrogance and sense of superiority which is at the same time shaky and sometimes aggressive. Mechanisms which keep a distance between the self and others will be used in order to protect this internal organisation.

Paranoid-schizoid mechanisms and relationships may be used in any situation where life and death anxieties abound. Isabel Menzies describes a hospital culture in the 1950s, in which rigid boundaries and hierarchies were built up in an attempt to avoid responsibility and grief. Patients were seen as 'the kidney in bed nine', having no existence before or outside the hospital. Nurses above the self in the hierarchy were typically idealised as either wonderful or dragons, while those below were seen as irresponsible and a danger to patients. Menzies-Lyth (1988) found that more mature nurses who were not prepared to split in this way tended to leave because they did not 'fit in'.

In a family facing illness or death, various splitting mechanisms may become evident: people and issues may be forgotten in a way they are not normally; feelings of being attacked and under threat may alternate with feelings of euphoria and unrealistic hopes. When the crisis is over some of these mechanisms will go out of use and the family will have to face feelings such as grief which were not experienced at the time of the emergency. Some of the grief will be attached to the cutting off which took place at the time and was felt to be destructive and damaging.

In general, the anxieties in the paranoid-schizoid position are life and death anxieties: you or me; my life or yours. Parents and children (or couples or workplaces) functioning in this way do not know how to share, how to care for each other; they each feel that they have to care for themselves since there is nobody else to care for them. A paranoid-schizoid atmosphere of distrust and suspicion, 'two-faced' placation and back-biting, erupting sometimes into open attack, can maintain itself. Any sign of care or love is likely to be interpreted by those around as weakness and be used against the caring person. Underlying this is a sense of total lack of love; there may be no conscious sense of loss and no awareness of a different way of functioning, except in terms of mockery or bitter triumph or cynicism.

Projective Identification

One of the ways the baby (and later the child) tries to deal with its own destructiveness is by disowning it. We know that adults often do this, attributing their own anger to someone else; fearing those they hate. The child does this too, experiencing his or her own aggression coming at him/herself from the outside; in particular, at first, the baby fears an attacking nipple and breast. Ernest Jones described a small boy who pointed to his mother's nipple when she began feeding his new brother, saying 'That's what you bit me with' (quoted by Susan Isaacs in King and Steiner, 1990: 313).

Klein described a mechanism she called projective identification which is used in the paranoid-schizoid position. Projection can be thought of as *perceiving* someone else as having one's own characteristics: projective identification involves a more active *getting rid of* something belonging to the self into someone else. Projective identification involves evoking in someone else aspects of the self which one cannot bear. It can be a very powerful means of communication of feelings (used by babies or small children before they can talk, for example). It can also be used as a destructive attack, with nasty or unbearable or 'mad' parts of the self evoked in other people in order to destroy their comfort, their peace of mind or their happiness.

Projective identification involves a very deep split, where the aspects of the self projected into others are very deeply denied in the self. In this way it differs from the more normal use of the word 'projection', where aspects of the self projected into others may more easily be discovered in the self. Where projective identification is used in excess, the recipient of the ejected parts of the self is not seen as being any more than a split-off part of the self: in this sense too it is destructive. In more normal forms of projection the other person may be perceived as having his or her own characteristics too: projection is less damaging in phantasy.

Klein first describes the process of projective identification as an attack on the mother:

The phantasied onslaughts on the mother follow two main lines: one is the predominantly oral impulse to suck dry, bite up, scoop out and rob the mother's body of its good contents . . . The other line of attack derives from the anal and urethral impulses and implies expelling dangerous substances (excrements) out of the self and into the mother. Together with these harmful excrements, expelled in hatred, split-off parts of the ego are also projected on to the mother or, as I would rather call it, into the mother. These excrements and bad parts of the self are meant not only to injure but also to control and take possession of the object. In so far as the mother comes to contain the bad parts of the self, she is not felt to be a separate individual but is felt to be the bad self.

Much of the hatred against parts of the self is now directed towards the mother. This leads to a particular form of identification which establishes the prototype of an aggressive object-relation. I suggest for these processes the term 'projective identification'. (Klein, 1975, III: 8)

In other words, in the child's phantasy, hated parts of the self are forced into the mother who is then identified with these parts of the self and hated violently.

Not only hated parts of the self may be got rid of into the mother in this way. Klein goes on to describe how good and loving parts of the self can also be projected into the mother. She points out that 'The projection of good feelings and good parts of the self into the mother is essential for the infant's ability to develop good object-relations and to integrate his ego. However, if this process is carried out excessively, good parts of the personality are felt to be lost.' The mother who is identified with a good part of the self in this way is idealised and therefore loses some of her more human, imperfect characteristics. 'Another consequence is the fear that the capacity to love has been lost because the loved object is felt to be loved predominantly as a representative of the self' (Klein, 1975, III: 9). The ability to love may also be felt to be part of the self projected into the mother in this way.

This concept of projective identification is crucial to the work of Kleinian analysts. The idea that parts of the self can be forced into others in phantasy has many ramifications, particularly in the context of psychoses. It was used by Segal in her study of symbol-formation and by Bion in his work on beta and alpha elements and the containing function of the mother and the analyst. These ideas will be explained in Chapter 5. It is basic to Kleinians' work with transference and counter-transference: the feelings which pass between analyst and patient. In a mild form it often illuminates marital and work relationships and relationships between adults and children on a day-to-day basis. In a gross form it can be particularly evident in people who suffered abuse as children. Therapists as well as other people can be provoked into some kind of re-enactment of the earlier abuse.

The Depressive Position

Klein identified the depressive position as a constellation of attitudes and phantasies which first appears when the baby is around 3 months of age. The tone of the baby's cry has changed by 3 months from a piercing scream to a more human sound and the baby can be seen to be relating differently to the mother and to the world around. By this age the baby can tolerate waiting for attention or food in a way which it could not at first: pain or tension does not simply have to be screamed out.

In the depressive position the baby (and later the child and adult) begins to integrate experience rather than to split it. Awareness of objects as more whole, with both loved and hated characteristics, begins. This has considerable consequences. Awareness of the self as a more whole, loving and hating being can also begin. Conflicts between different parts of the self are no longer solved by splitting and pushing those parts into others, including the good object itself, but by holding them within the self.

In the paranoid-schizoid position the absence of the good breast/mother is experienced as the presence of a bad and frightening one (as darkness is experienced as the presence of something tangible and frightening, rather than simply the loss of light). Loss of the mother in the first months of life may be felt as extreme pain in the stomach, for example, but cannot be kept in the mind as a thought or memory. An unthinkable thought is experienced as a physical pain. Once the baby reaches the depressive position, thoughts and thinking provide a means of holding onto a mental representation of the absent mother as good.

With a fairly well-established idea of the distinction between goodness and badness, the baby can begin to see both in the same mother/breast without one destroying the other and the mother/breast with it. Disappointment with the mother does not turn her into something wholly bad and dangerous: damage is no longer feared as total destruction. A good experience does not mean heaven forever; its loss is not the end of the world but is a real, manageable grief mitigated by hope for good experiences in the future. The internal mother-object is seen as more resilient to attack as well as both loved and hated. In this way the baby gradually achieves a sense of internal strength; such a good object is ultimately a source of support throughout life. The sense of the mother holding the baby in mind grows with the sense that the baby can hold the mother in mind. All of this brings with it the awareness of loss, grief, sadness and mourning.

Guilt, too, makes its appearance in the depressive position, as the baby realises that the breast/mother it loves is the same as the one it attacks. Jealousy arises as the price of awareness that the loved object can be cared for by someone else, but mitigated in good circumstances by the benefits of being loved by this other person. The sense of the self as the centre of the loved object's world is challenged and changes, which raises the possibility of separation of the self from the object/mother in a way which would not destroy either. These elements of the depressive position show the link between Oedipal anxieties and an awareness of reality, both internal and external. We shall now look at some of these elements of the depressive position in more detail, showing how they apply in later life.

In the paranoid-schizoid position, anxieties are connected with survival, with fears of persecution, annihilation and suffocation; being taken over or swallowed up. In the depressive position, the main source of anxiety is for the object: real care and concern for the loved breast in its 'not me' aspect, can begin, Klein thought, as early as 3 months. In moments of contact with reality the baby is aware of having attacked the breast, later the mother, and of a great longing to repair the damage. However, the breast to the baby at first is close to being the baby's whole world, and the baby also becomes aware of a sense of being too small and incomplete to be able to repair the damage to such an enormous breast/mother alone. It is this concern which motivates the search for a father: someone who will protect the mother *from the baby's own attacks*. This solution to the conflict brings with it the pain of jealousy but, as a young man said to me once, 'I'd rather be jealous than trapped.' The alternative is being trapped into a never-ending dependent relationship with a huge, demanding mother-figure. The Oedipal struggles take place within this context: however much the child (of either sex) wants to take the place of the father with the mother, it is desperately important to the child that someone else should have the primary responsibility for her.

Under the pressure of frustrations of various kinds, the attacks of the paranoid-schizoid position continue throughout life, though mitigated more and more by a sense of love and reality which can no longer be totally denied. As a result, there is always psychic work to do, undoing some of the damage of these cuts. Adults at times show new awareness of the way they have ill-treated others such as their parents or a past lover, for example, by mockery or thoughtless rejection or attacks of some other kind. This recognition brings both guilt and sense of loss, but also a new chance to relate differently to people in the future; a better chance of holding and keeping love relationships. This is part of the maturing process. Joyce Grenfell, the comedian, described how she found it increasingly hard to laugh at people as she grew older and began to realise why they were the way they were.

Relationships under paranoid-schizoid conditions may be alternately clinging and rejecting, with caring experienced as invasive and suffocating. Erna at 6 was described by Klein as completely dominating her mother, allowing her no freedom of movement and plaguing her continually with her love and hatred; Erna's mother said 'She swallows me up.' This is very different from the caring of the depressive position. True caring and sharing in adult life depend on the satisfactory negotiation of the pain and anxieties of the depressive position: tolerance of jealousy and separateness rather than a furiously destructive reaction to them which attacks love or the loved person. In order to be able to care and share, others have to be seen as human beings with their own characteristics, rather than simply parts of the self. Parts of the self as well as parts of earlier loved objects continue throughout life to be invested in others; as these parts become less idealised (good or bad) and less monstrous, the need to deny them so totally in the self lessens. This reinforces the sense of sharing the same world as other people and can strengthen real caring.

Changes in the relationship to a good object are also sometimes observed in marriages. An adult functioning under the influence of paranoid-schizoid anxieties has no idea of a loss of a good wife or husband, once loved, but is only aware of the presence of a bad, cruel attacking one. Therapy sometimes brings awareness of what has been lost and the possibility of mourning it, enabling a more loving relationship to emerge.

Klein saw the conflict between love and hatred as the motive force for much of what happens in life. The earliest relation with the father and other people is partly motivated by a need to find ways of dealing with aggressive phantasies directed at the mother and her breast. The need to find a new partner to replace the mother is motivated by conflicts in the relation with the mother. Creative work of all kinds symbolises an attempt to restore the breast, attacked and damaged by the baby in infancy. In the depressive position these conflicts can be worked on in a way which does not increase the damage but is creative and loving, allowing the development of caring relationships with others as well as with the self.

Objects and Part-objects

Unlike Freud and some other analysts, Klein did not believe that there is a period during which the child only relates to itself. One of the baby's first actions is to search for the nipple: the baby is born in some sense aware of the need for something outside itself.

Klein considered that even a narcissistic relationship with one's own body which is characteristic of a very small baby or child (and of some adults) depends on a more primitive love relationship with a breast/mother which has been taken in and identified with the self in phantasy. She often described children in analysis eating pieces of paper or drinking from a tap, for example, which they had previously designated as some part of their mother or father. They showed her in many different ways that they believed they had taken their parents and parts of their parents' bodies inside them.

Klein thought that the baby's original love-object was the mother's breast, though it was a breast endowed with all kinds of meaning which went far beyond that of a mammary gland producing milk. Klein found that phantasies of the breast included the breast as a source of all life, love and hope, of babies and good things, of comfort, peace and serenity. She found phantasies of the baby getting inside it or taking it in and fusing with it in a blissful state. However, she also found phantasies of being eaten up by it, torn apart or threatened by it; of the breast being damaged or dangerously bad, inside or outside the baby. These primitive phantasies belonged to the paranoid-schizoid position.

To begin with, babies do not know that the mother's breast is irrevocably attached to her and could not survive without her: to see other aspects of the mother as separate from the breast at first is not unreasonable, given the knowledge available to a new baby. As the baby grows, if conditions are good, it begins to recognise that the breast belongs to the mother and is part of her and not of the baby self. This takes place under the influence of the depressive position.

However, the depressive position is not comfortable, and at times of stress the child or adult may attempt to get rid of the new awareness that it brings. Klein found that children also had phantasies of cutting up and cutting off parts of the parents' bodies, and this also created part-objects out of more whole ones.

In Richard's analysis a 'nice Mrs Klein' was cut out of the whole perception of her and kept separate from the 'bad Mrs Klein' who was attributed to the cook. In the paranoid-schizoid position, one-dimensional, one-characteristic part-objects created in this way are often used as a 'solution' to internal conflict. By splitting his perception of Klein, Richard could temporarily satisfy his desire to have a nice analyst while actually being suspicious of her: the cost was to his integrity and his long-term security. Not only

Cinderella's step-mother and fairy-godmother, but also many Hollywood film characters are part-objects in this sense. Adults also generally relate to politicians or other public figures as part-objects: for example, expecting them to behave better than ordinary human beings even though they know on one level that they really are ordinary human beings.

These part-objects serve the purpose of avoiding (rather than working through) internal conflict and guilt. Children (and adults) have many conflicts which they try to solve by splitting their perception of the people involved. These cut-up people, however, are ultimately to be feared and distrusted. The splitting process was seen by Klein as an attack not only on the person concerned but also on the perception of reality; as such it is itself a danger to long-term security.

The story of Cinderella offers a young girl triumph over adult women; but as a model for a real woman or girl it is lacking. It expresses a little girl's vicious envy towards her mother, creating a monstrous step-mother and daughters in the process and leaving Cinderella herself quite unrealistically 'good'. The bad figures are multiplied as well as split: the idealised fairy-godmother is unreal. Given the level of destructiveness expressed, it is not surprising that a small girl should prefer not to own it, but to see herself instead as the Cinderella victim.

The creation of part-objects in this way is an illustration of Klein's belief that idealisation is a defence against persecutory phantasies rather than reality. A small girl's own envy and jealousy of her mother is painful reality: in her attempts to get rid of this she creates Cinderella's envious step-mother, a persecutory phantasy. The fairy-godmother and Cinderella, as a helpless innocent victim, are both idealisations which then defend the girl from this phantasy woman.

Where the paranoid-schizoid position deals in part-objects, under the influence of the depressive position the infant becomes much more aware of whole objects, in which characteristics felt to be good and loved coexist with characteristics felt to be bad, hated and feared. At the same time the child (or adult) feels more whole and more human, sharing both good and bad characteristics and conflicts with others.

Reality would require a small girl to reinstate her envied mother and suffer the fact that her parents have their own lives and a sexual relationship and that she must wait for adulthood herself: the gain would be that she no longer had to sit in the cinders or to deny herself a real mother. She would also have to see the injustice of her view of her mother as an envious, wicked step-mother, and her own culpability when it came to envious and jealous attacks. Regaining awareness of her own envy and jealousy would bring at the same time both guilt and loss (of idealisation of herself) and an increase in her sense of her own strength and her closeness to her real mother. The reduction in splitting allows for sharing the guilt of jealousy and of more human failings; and a corresponding reduction in the glorious isolation of Cinderella left behind at the hearth while her wicked family are out enjoying themselves.

It may also be clear that a girl needs help to reach this level of maturity. While she feels that her own envious and jealous fury makes her totally monstrous and beyond the pale, she cannot integrate this perception of herself, but can only get rid of it into someone else. She needs the help of a loving adult to enable her to recognise that her badness is tolerable, if she is successfully to negotiate the depressive position.

Internal and External Objects

Klein distinguished between the external mother and phantasies of the mother both inside and outside the self. Part of the process of development involves the building up of a resilient internal mother-figure, a 'good object', which can survive attack, be the object of love and care, and provide a sense of being loved and cared for. This good internal mother-figure is built up not only out of real experiences of being loved (not just by the mother but by other people too), but also out of the child's experience of loving. This internal mother gives a sense of being grounded, of security, of goodness which can be given as well as received.

When children call their teacher 'mum' or their mother 'miss' they are demonstrating how the internal good mother-phantasy is used to relate to and understand other women as well as the mother. This is why good relations with a step-mother (or even a foster-mother, a therapist or a lover) can enhance the relationship with the mother rather than spoil it. Good feelings with one mother-figure carry over into the relationship with other mother-figures. Bad ones do too. Children do sometimes split parents and step-parents into good and bad but this is itself a result of bad relations carrying over. The 'good' relationship in such a pair is likely to be idealised rather than true and firm, covering a sense of persecution and perhaps clearly hypocritical at times. The 'bad' relationship is likely to be known to be unfair and exaggerated and may later swing round into an idealisation, while the original 'good' relationship is denigrated.

In addition to this sense of a good, powerfully loving internal mother/breast figure, the child has a sense of many other internal objects too. Bad ones tend to be more numerous and less integrated, as one of the ways a child tries to deal with bad objects in phantasy is to chop them up and scatter them. Bad internal objects may be very frightening since they have no loving or caring aspects to modify them. The good internal mother/breast is more human and complex and closer to reality.

The process of loving and losing caring and cared-for people is crucial to the development of a resilient and strong internal good object. During the process of loss, phantasies of the goodness of the object may be under attack. The child who says 'she wasn't worth having anyway' or 'I'm better than she is' in response to losing his mother's attention to a new brother, for example, has not only lost his external mother but has also denigrated his phantasy internal mother. Attacks on the actual mother in the external world as a result of such denigration may either bring retaliatory attacks or understanding and help, depending on the mother's own mental state and the amount of internal and external support she experiences from loved objects herself.

It is only when the pain of grief can be withstood that the child or adult can say 'She was good and I've lost her.' Children need adults who care for them if they are to maintain a belief that 'inside me I can feel she still loves me.' Without this their belief in the existence of a loving self and in their own ability to love without destroying is under threat. Fathers often provide this help; the mother herself (particularly by her acknowledgement and understanding of the child's feelings) may too.

When conditions are good the child is able to be aware of an internal mother/breast with a certain amount of independence of the child; allowed to have something the child does not have and the capacity to give it to the child. An internal mother-figure like this, felt to have an existence of her own and not entirely dependent upon the child's wishes and moods, can be felt as a support to the child, nourishing the child throughout life.

Development of Sexuality

Klein agreed with Freud that the original relationship with the mother was the basis for later sexual and marital relationships. She differed from Freud in her belief that the child was aware very early on of the existence of the penis and the vagina. She thought children have an innate awareness of the genitals just as they have an innate awareness of a breast and nipple. She also differed from

Freud (and some present-day analysts) in her belief that the baby, child and adult at depth seek someone who is different from themselves and has something more to offer, not just a repeat of an earlier relationship with themselves.

Klein saw feeding experiences as the basis for genital sexual feelings as well as believing that there was an innate awareness of the sexual act and its meaning. Where feeding phantasies have been predominately good, the phantasies governing sexual relationships will be predominately good. Sex will be understood as a mutual gratification, a good relationship in which each partner feeds and is fed by the other emotionally as well as in the giving and taking of genital pleasure. 'Something good' can be felt to come out of the relationship: whether it is babies or some other kind of creativity in which both partners are enriched. The adult erect penis is in relative size for the adult close to the size of the nipple for the baby; the vagina can be 'understood' as a warm, loving mouth: this gives deep and resonant meaning to sexual activities of all kinds. In phantasy, the attachment of sexual organs to the people they belong to will be firm and valued.

Phantasies used to understand genital sex also include bad ones. Fears of the damage done by the mouth to the nipple or breast may spill over into fears of the damage which could be done to the penis by the vagina or to the inside of the woman's body by the penis. Fears of the penis being bitten off and retained by the woman inside her during sex are also common amongst children. Sexual organs can in phantasy be cut off from their owners, as in some crude jokes. People may be rejected and only their sexual organs desired. Instead of love, loving and creativity, sexuality may be understood to produce destructiveness, damage and a diminishing of both partners. Such phantasies may be disproved by life experiences, or they may seem to be confirmed. They may be self-fulfilling prophecies or they may simply fit bad experiences over which the individual had no control at all.

Where the relationship with the mother has not been good for any reason, the baby's own genitals can be used by the baby to distract from terrifyingly bad phantasies. It seems that some babies turn to their genitals earlier and with a greater intensity than others. The genitals can be used to create a sense of the circle being closed; of all pleasure and need being satisfied by the self. Masturbatory pleasure can be used to deny the need for a relationship with another real person: a relationship which may not have been available or which may have been rejected. Underneath this idealisation of the baby's own ability to satisfy itself are hidden very disturbing phantasies of attacks on the object which does not provide the gratification desired. (Drugs including alcohol and nicotine can also be used in a similar way.)

Klein found that masturbation in childhood could involve very sadistic and cruel fantasies directed at parents felt as neglectful: some of the guilt children normally feel towards masturbation may be attached to such fantasies. She found that children often make themselves give up masturbation out of a considerable sense of guilt and fear of damage even when adults have never expressed any objection to it. She also described instances of children involved in sexual relations with brothers and sisters, and traced some of the very distressing phantasies and the unconscious guilt the children felt in connection with this, whether they were the victim or the aggressor or both. In a very early paper ('Criminal Tendencies in Normal Children', 1927; Klein, 1975, vol. I) she described criminal acts arising out of such abuse.

This is quite different from the way a happy small boy of 18 months used his genitals, attempting to put his penis in his mother's ear and mouth and trying to rub it against her playfully while she prevented him, both laughing. Here the genital phantasies are clearly developed from loving ones: to do with an attempt to feed the mother with his 'nipple'; probably to give the mother babies; to make something good to share with the mother not just to have for the self alone. Similarly, a 5-year-old girl snuggled her genitals and her legs against her mother in a very sexual way and was clearly hurt when her mother pushed her off. In such situations, the way the mother refuses such advances is important in allowing the child to feel their impulses are permissible but also safely limited by the adults around.

Children identify alternately with both parents: disappointment with one pushes them to identify with the other: this too will fail and the process repeats. Gradually, they are forced to disentangle themselves from their parents and to establish their own separate identity with their own separate partners who have the advantages of being neither their mother nor their father. This aspect of sexuality will be taken up in the next section.

In good circumstances, the child may turn from both parents towards its genitals only occasionally. More of the phantasies attached to the genitals will be of a loving and feeding kind in which goodness and pleasure are being shared. Later when the baby becomes an adult the fear of sex and the harm it can do will be outweighed not by an overvaluation of it (covering a fear) but by a realistic conviction that good babies and a good loving relationship can be created and held, not lost. Some fear will be present but this will be accessible and will be modifiable by the reassurance of good sexual experience and ultimately, if conditions are favourable, by the birth of healthy babies.

(The birth of a baby 'with something wrong' is difficult not simply for realistic reasons but also because it may be taken as evidence that damage has been done to the inside of the woman's body by her mother (in retaliation for her phantasied attacks on her mother's ability to have babies) or by the sexual act itself: both new parents may have their earliest anxieties awakened by such an event, making it hard for them to cope with the baby and parent-hood. Particularly where this is a first baby, the anxieties can be enormously strong and the relationship between the parents can be under threat.)

In less favourable circumstances the child who turns in hatred to its own genitals may as an adult use its genitals in the service of hatred and cruelty towards the self and others.

Fathers

In the depressive position, the baby becomes aware of someone else taking the good object away at times; generally of a father-object which comes between baby and breast and deprives it of the breast. In addition, by his relation with the mother, the father-figure takes away the illusion of mother–child unity and completeness. Jealousy and rivalry emerge as the baby learns to handle three-people rela-tionships. The father (or other person such as a sibling) who takes the mother away may become the repository for some of the baby's own destructive and damaging feelings. In addition, the father in another phantasy comes to represent the child's reparative and creative impulses, creating new possibilities for helping the baby to manage its destructive impulses. By introjecting a helpful and loving father who cares for the mother, the child takes in a power-ful new set of phantasies which are very important particularly when it comes to separating from the mother, growing up and leaving home.

Freud thought that a girl wanted her father primarily to give her a penis for herself, in order that she could be a man. Elizabeth Spillius (1988) says that many of Freud's patients were young women with what we now call conversion symptoms: present-day understanding is that such women very often idealise and desire a penis for themselves and are denigrating towards their mothers and towards men as love objects. Freud's theory would apply to these women. (Conversion symptoms are symptoms created by the con-version of emotional feelings into physical ones: a stomach ache instead of an anxiety-provoking thought, for example, or a paralysis of the hand instead of an acknowledgement of anxieties connected with writing cheques.)

Klein, however, had a much wider view. She was certain that girls wanted their fathers as love-objects and not simply as possessions. She felt that in good circumstances loving phantasies, derived from the relationship with the breast as an object of desire and affection, were the foundation for loving phantasies of the father as well as of the mother. Other people too, such as brothers and sisters, nurses and grandparents, could also be experienced by the child as a source of love and comfort in themselves.

Love for people other than the mother is observable from very early on. Klein thought that it arises in several ways. Love for the breast and love experienced from the breast 'spills over' into love for the whole world and all in it. In particular, the baby feels love and gratitude towards the mother's partner and others felt to be supporting and caring for her. These people are seen as allies in the task of restoring her and repairing the damage done to her in phantasy. In good circumstances, the baby hopes that these people will restore the mother who has been depleted and exhausted by the baby, both in phantasy and to some extent in reality too. This love may be tinged with envy or with gratitude, depending how the baby feels about life in general and its own lack of ability to restore her single-handedly.

Love for the father or siblings may also arise in a different way. If the relation with the mother has been felt to be too frustrating and unsatisfying, the baby may turn to the father as part of an attack on the mother. This often happens in a mild way at a time of increased separation between mother and baby, if she goes back to work leaving the baby, or weans it or has another baby. If the love for the mother/breast is well established, the anger with her and preference for the father (so often visible in a small girl) is underpinned with love and concern for both. If this love is less secure and the child turns to the father in an attempt to escape a truly destructive relationship with the mother, this hatred eventually emerges in the relationship with the father too. The child may in turn reject the father and turn back to the mother, idealising her in an attempt to deny the underlying hatred. The cut-off bad relationship continues to affect the child and may be played out elsewhere.

The baby may also turn to the father if it is furious with the mother out of envy of the mother's superior capacities. The father may be loved more precisely because he does not have the breast and the capacity to have babies 'inside' as the mother does, and therefore does not arouse such envy. He may also be felt, like the child, to be deprived by the mother. The price for this love may be a need to keep him perceived as lacking his own real potency too.

Fathers are also felt to come between the baby and the breast, separating them and destroying phantasies of fusion with an internal and external mother/breast. This may be a source of frustration and anger but ultimately it also helps to establish a sense of separateness and space for the baby as well as for the mother, keeping them from becoming too close and too muddled up and trapped in each other.

Fathers, like mothers, also provide a model for the child him/herself as well as for a sexual partner. The child takes in his/her father in phantasy and then may identify with him or attempt to create an identity in opposition to him, out of fear of being like him. A father by his behaviour may, for example, reassure the child that firmness, authority and love can mutually coexist. Equally he may convince the child that authority means cruelty and love means rejection and victimisation. He may combine weakness with irritability and demands on his wife which rival the child's; the child will take this in too. Where a child is trying to create his or her own identity without a good parental model, he or she may have considerable difficulty. In the absence of a good father, children will create a phantasy idealised one, often based on their views of a father at the age they were when he left. Their anger towards this abandoning father may make the negative phantasies very frightening. Equally, people who are constantly trying *not* to be like an actual parent may appear false and superficial because they cannot behave spontaneously for fear of betraying themselves. Identification with the phantasy internal father cannot be avoided but may in this case be denied, which creates a sense of some part of the self being cut off.

As we said before, fathers are often the focus of the child's destructive phantasies. The 'burglar under the bed', or thief who will break in and steal, later, a rapist feared, may well be a version of an attacking father-phantasy, made up partly out of real experience and partly out of the child's own fears of their own desires to break into their mother's body, take her babies and make her suffer forever. (Trude, described in the next chapter, expressed such phantasies in her play.) Destructiveness originally experienced or phantasised to and from the mother may be attributed to the father in an attempt to 'protect' the relationship with the mother. The cost is idealisation and weakening of the mother–child relationship.

Where fathers are actually violent, children in phantasy may understand this as an expression of their own secret violent feelings. This may make it extremely hard for them to admit what is happening or to resist effectively: children's sense of responsibility for their parent's behaviour has many roots, but this is one of them. Their beliefs about their own aggression are deeply affected by their witnessing of their parent's behaviour. The effect may be to encourage very deep splits in children's perception of themselves: they may find it extremely difficult to control their own aggression except by denying it. They may thus become, like their parent, vulnerable to sudden eruptions of violence, uncontrolled by their reality sense. They may play out violent scenarios with other adults or with children in an attempt to seek some reassurance about their actual capacity for violence and the damage they can cause.

Fathers, in Klein's view, are more important to children than people often recognise. Absent fathers continue to play an enormous part in children's fantasy worlds, both conscious and unconscious. When they leave they confirm some of the children's terrifying phantasies about themselves and their own destructiveness. The relation with them and with those aspects of the self which they represent for the child continues to influence the child's view of the world; but these phantasies may not be free to develop as they would if the father were there. Children who have lost a parent at any age often show clear signs of retaining phantasies from that time. Their view of fathers, for example, may never have grown past the view that they had when their father left them, for whatever reason. These views are generally quite unrealistic and sometimes (though not always) prevent the child from making fulfilling relationships with partners later.

In Klein's view, fathers are understood initially with phantasies which have their origin in the relation with the mother. These include deeply loving phantasies; phantasies in which the father is an ally and aid in mending the damage the child fears it has done; and phantasies in which the father stands for the child's own aggressiveness. The behaviour of the actual father is of enormous importance in helping children with their phantasies about men and about themselves and their relation with their mother too. His ability to take on, to represent and to control the child's aggressiveness without being taken over by it is important: his ability to come between child and mother while giving something good to both, and his own character as a model for the child, contributing something of himself to the child's world, all affect the child's development.

Babies

Freud thought that, at depth, girls wanted babies as a substitute for the penis they did not have: in other words, primarily as part of their relationship with themselves and their own bodies. Klein thought that girls under normal conditions wanted babies for much more complex reasons. She thought that if they did want them as substitutes for a penis of their own then this was pathological and would not be the basis for a good relationship with the baby.

Many women, Klein thought, under the influence of the depressive position, want babies because in phantasy they want to restore to their mothers the babies they damaged in her in phantasy when they were small, but they are hopeful of being able to do this with help from a man. They want a baby as part of a loving relationship, confirming the goodness of the bond between two different people, representing on a deep level baby-self and breast/mother; and their own self in relation to their own loved parents. They enjoy and value the difference between the sexes, between themselves and their partner, just as they were able to enjoy and value the difference between themselves and the breast/mother and between their parents. They want a baby to love and care for as on a deep level they feel they have been loved and cared for.

Some women, under the influence of more paranoid-schizoid anxieties, do as Freud thought want a baby to decorate themselves, to triumph over their own mothers and other people; to show the world that they are 'all right' and have everything: but Klein saw this as a cover-up for phantasies of being empty and having nothing inside. Women like this may not have a phantasy of a good mother and a supportive and good father who can restore and be restored, love and be loved. Their feeling that they must have everything and be entirely independent covers a despair that they have been left on their own, either through their own rejection of mothering or because their mother did not provide them with what they needed. Such a woman wants a baby to love her as she feels nobody ever loved her.

If the mother's despair of making relationships with real people is too great this can cause difficulties for the baby. Since phantasies derived from the breast/mother are used to understand the baby, a mother who has no hope about relating to a separate breast/mother/partner may only be able to relate to the baby if it is seen as part of her and its own difference squashed.

In happier circumstances the baby will at times represent some part of the mother without being completely identified with it. All mothers probably see themselves in their babies at times: at other times they may see the baby as standing for their own loved and loving internal mother. They may also see the baby at times as standing for a persecuting and demanding internal mother-figure: bigger than the mother herself and sucking her dry. Mothering can be exhausting, and such phantasies both express and contribute to the exhaustion. Some mothers can also at times see their baby as a person in its own right. Babies allowed their own existence in this way may have a better chance of growing up with a firm sense of a loved self, able to use and enjoy temporary identification with other people but less constrained to fit in with someone else's view of them all of the time.

Anxiety

In Freud's earlier writings he describes anxiety as deriving from inhibited sexuality. Frustrated sexual feelings, he thought, were converted into feelings of anxiety. Later, in 'Inhibitions, Symptoms and Anxiety' (1926) he changed this view and linked anxiety to a fear of the loss of the object: originally the mother who protects the baby from the danger of 'being hopelessly exposed to an unpleasurable tension due to instinctual need'. Later this transforms into fear of loss of the penis which he describes as an organ which would allow the child to 'be once more united to his mother – i.e. to a substitute for her – in the act of copulation' (Freud, 1975, XX: 139). Still later this is modified into a fear of the super-ego, and later still, into 'a fear of death (or fear for life) which is a fear of the super-ego projected on to the powers of destiny'.

Klein's views about anxiety, like Freud's, evolved. At first she followed Freud and Ernest Jones in attributing anxiety to the fear of castration or fear of loss of the capacity for sexual pleasure. However, in 1933 in her paper 'The Early Development of Conscience in the Child', she describes persecutory anxiety as arising from the child's fear of its own aggressive impulses.

These aggressive impulses she saw as instinctual. Developing Freud's ideas, she saw them as arising from a 'death instinct' which was in conflict with its opposite, a 'life instinct', from the very beginning. The effect of the life instinct was to redirect aggression from life itself towards an external object, initially the mother's breast. Rather than hating life and the self, the baby turned its hatred onto the mother. This is illustrated by Hanna Segal when she describes a patient who saved himself from suicide by a fantasy of killing his analyst (H. Segal, in preparation). This is discussed further in Chapter 4.

Klein observed small children's fear of attacks by a revengeful mother/breast figure on the inside of the child's own body, and on the organs of sexual pleasure. This fear gave a quality to anxiety which she called 'persecutory': later, she saw it as part of the paranoid-schizoid position. It can lead to attempts to get rid of the anxiety into someone else; for example, a child may make the mother or another child feel persecutory anxiety in an attempt to get rid of the unbearable feeling.

In addition, Klein distinguished the 'depressive' anxiety of the depressive position, in which the fear has moved to fears for the good breast/mother's safety. This anxiety has a different quality to it. Depressive anxiety is more bearable than persecutory anxiety. It involves recognition of the goodness of the lost loved person and awareness of pining, grief and guilt. Depressive anxiety can be held within the self and is a stimulus to attempt to make things better: on one level, to apologise or express sorrow; on another level, to attempt some kind of reparation. Through symbolic reparation anxiety of a bearable kind becomes a stimulus to creative work.

Anxiety plays an important role in Kleinian theory and practice. It is by seeking the source of a present anxiety and modifying it that an analyst brings relief to a patient. It is anxiety which may either prevent or motivate change. Mechanisms such as splitting, disintegration and denial take place under the pressure of persecutory anxieties; while, on the other hand, integration and acceptance of reality may be ways of dealing with depressive anxieties.

Klein originally thought that anxiety prevented development, and excessive anxiety does. However, she showed later in 'The Importance of Symbol Formation in the Development of the Ego' (Klein, 1975, vol. I) that development depends on tolerating and working through anxiety. Where anxiety is simply expelled, it is not available to create the necessary conditions for change within the psyche.

Envy

In *Envy and Gratitude* (Klein, 1975, vol. III) Klein listed some of the ways in which people can attack goodness and love *because it is* goodness and love. Clearly, this is a radical and powerful idea. She distinguished between envy and jealousy; envy she saw as a relationship between the infant, the envied person and the envied characteristic or possession. Jealousy is a relationship between the infant and two other people, one of whom the infant loves and the other of whom seems to the infant to be receiving the love which the infant wants and who becomes the object of hatred, anger and rivalry. Envy is spoiling and damaging in nature, neatly expressed in 'throwing shit' at someone or something. Jealousy retains a sense of the goodness of the loved object. Envy is characteristic of the paranoid-schizoid position; jealousy requires the sophistication of the depressive position. Klein thought that many adult difficulties arose out of envy. She felt it was rightly considered to be the worst sin, since it attacks all virtue and all enjoyment and pleasure in life.

Towards the end of her life she became convinced that envy was innate and that people were born with different capacities for envy and gratitude. She considered envy as one of the factors limiting the effectiveness of analysis. Since envy destroys pleasure in the self as well as in others, the benefits of truth and understanding cannot be enjoyed by the envious person. In addition, she thought that split-off envious parts of the mind may be constantly in struggle with less envious parts. The envious part may not allow happiness, creativity and success for anyone.

Symbolism

Freud's work on dreams led him to recognise the importance of symbolism. He found how easily we transfer thoughts and feelings from one object to another. Klein took this up and discovered that the whole process went much further. Freud speaks of symbols in a way which makes them appear rather *ad hoc*, so an umbrella or a walking stick, for example, may symbolise a penis, and a house or room a mother, but it is not terribly clear why or how. Klein's theory of phantasy and reality-testing makes the whole issue much clearer.

In Klein's theory, phantasies are an important aspect of a child's attempt to make sense of the world. Phantasies of restoring the world and the parents to a blissful state, of loving and creating, of people and things in states of great pleasure and happiness giving each other wonderful gifts of love are going on all the time. So too are phantasies of being devoured and devouring, being torn to pieces and tearing with fingernails, being bitten up and biting. The conflicts between phantasies give rise to many anxieties. One of the functions of the ego is to search the external world for information, and a vital part of the information sought is some kind of confirmation or refutation of anxiety-filled phantasies. Symbolism develops out of the search for representatives in the external world of objects in the internal one.

In other words, the child is searching for damaged or healthy penises, nipples and breasts; mothers and fathers who are whole and loving or split off, damaged and revengeful. The penis and fingers are found in the search for a child's own nipple; the father is used in the search for a representative of split-off aspects of the mother and self; a teacher or older sibling may be found to fill a phantasy of an attacking, bullying, scornful parent/self who knows everything and wants to humiliate the child/self who knows nothing.

The reason why it is so easy to find symbols for breasts, penises, faeces, fathers and mothers is that we constantly relate to the world on this level at the same time as on more mature levels. These were the elements that interested us passionately as babies, and which gave rise to our deepest anxieties. If we are looking for examples of penises or breasts, it is easy enough to see them everywhere. If we are looking for evidence of our own competence or incompetence, our lovability or failure, we can quite easily endow things and people around us with a relevant meaning, with more or less respect for the way they actually are, depending how in touch we are with reality.

Symbols develop with the development of the child. In the *Narrative of a Child Analysis* we can trace the different symbolic ways in which Richard represented his mother and Klein. The most primitive representations of his mother included the colour light blue, circles representing breasts, a station, and the building he was in. More mature symbols for the mother were people Richard saw through the window and the cook, as well as Klein herself. The characteristic of 'being alive' is in contrast to being inanimate or immovable and therefore controllable, and implies some ability to tolerate the reality of other people's separate existence. To create such symbols, he had integrated his view of his mother sufficiently to understand her as a person but had then split her into a nice mummy and a nasty cook. This illustrates the results in symbolism of the alternation between depressive integration and paranoid-schizoid splitting.

The symbolism in adult anxieties suggests that they are not so far from babies' anxieties as described by Klein. We worry about the quality of our work: do we simply produce 'shit' or can we produce something as good as a baby: a creative work of art, or a solid piece of work which can stand on its merits, with a life of its own? Is it our own or stolen from or by someone else? Can we control those we love or will they still love us if we allow them to go free? Were we fed good food or was it poison? Are we offered a useful theory, good food for the mind, or a dangerous, secretly destructive one? As therapists are we making people better or are we damaging them? Did our efforts to love and protect our mothers/children/clients work or were they simply more subtle forms of attack? We may watch these people anxiously to see how they are surviving under our ministrations just as when we were small we watched our parents to see how they survived.

Psychotic Conditions

Klein's view of the possibility of analysing people suffering from schizophrenia was extremely radical. When she analysed Dick, childhood schizophrenia was not yet recognised. She also briefly analysed a schizophrenic woman. This convinced her that such analysis was possible. She thought that there was a sane part of the personality which could ally with the therapist as well as a psychotic or mad part which aimed to destroy sanity.

Once abnormal situations have sharpened observations, it may become easier to see processes which otherwise would have remained hidden. Klein had thought for a long time that psychotic processes were part of normal development; her analysis of Dick illuminated both the normality and abnormality of psychoses. She thought that psychotic processes, a cutting off of awareness of reality, was part of normal development; but in some people an excess of both sadism and empathy for the object caused these mechanisms to be over-used to an extent that was extremely damaging to development.

In her work with Dick she found enormous sadism and cruelty which he feared would destroy his mother as well as himself. Along with this sadism he also had a very strong empathy for his mother, though he was somewhat confused about this because he could not use symbols correctly to distinguish between people and things which represented them. His first play with the toys three days after his analysis began was to convey to Klein that he wanted her to cut some pieces of wood out of a toy truck: he then proceeded to throw this out of the room and then to hide it at the bottom of the drawer. It was his very powerful desire to cut things out of and to attack his mother and things representing her, together with his enormous fear of this sadism, which had made him too frightened to use knives or scissors correctly, or even to protect himself when he fell over. This level of sadism and anxiety about it, she believed, was a feature of psychosis.

'Psychotic' means being cut off from reality, and the word 'cut' is highly appropriate. The cuts of psychosis are deep and cruel attacks on the self, on loved objects and on the organs of perception themselves. Alongside this cutting there is an equally strong longing to make things right again: but every attempt to repair seems to repeat the damage. The correspondingly high levels of anxiety involved make it both difficult and risky to work with people like this. The risk of damage to the self and others is real: analysis raises anxieties while helping the person to deal with them in a different way, and psychotic anxieties in particular need to be firmly contained in a safe situation.

Klein's descriptions of the paranoid-schizoid position and projective identification are essential for an understanding of analysis of psychotic phantasies. Her belief that an excess of empathy is as important as an excess of sadism is typical of her ability to detect the loving side of even very destructive phantasies and states of mind. Her conviction that within the most crazy person was a sane part of the mind which could be contacted was equally typical of her.

In *Envy and Gratitude* Klein wrote for the first time of split-off archaic parts of the self which needed to remain split off. She thought that if these split-off archaic objects suddenly erupt into consciousness a psychotic breakdown could be precipitated. Klein does not mention drugs, but it seems that some of the mind-influencing drugs such as LSD may cause this kind of breakdown. Chapter 5 takes up some of the explorations of psychoses undertaken by Bion and other students of Klein.

3

Klein's Major Practical Contributions

Klein's major practical contributions have been in the field of psychoanalysis in general and child analysis in particular. In the analysis of psychotic processes, Klein's contribution was particularly outstanding.

Klein's work with adults used insights she had obtained in her work with children. Similarly, counsellors and therapists today use insights developed by Klein in the very different context of psychoanalysis. This chapter describes the practical lessons Klein drew from her work, and illustrates them, as Klein discovered them, through her work with children.

Play Therapy

Klein's method of analysing children was based on her discovery that their play could be interpreted in the same way that dreams could in adults. She described her technique in Chapter 2 of *The Psychoanalysis of Children* (Klein, 1975, vol. II). She provided children with a room in which they could freely express themselves; small toys which could be used imaginatively; paper, scissors and pencils, water and containers. This room and its contents became part of the tools with which her child patients showed Klein how they felt about themselves and their world. Klein entered into this world with the minimum of restrictions, though she did prevent the children from physically damaging either themselves or her. She interpreted the children's anxieties in a sympathetic way, taking full account of the powerful conflicts they suffered between the rival demands of love and hatred, truth and illusion.

This was entirely new. Play therapy has been taken up since by many analysts, but by no means all follow Klein's lead in offering interpretations of the kind and in the way she did. Play therapy carries over into work with adults by drawing attention to the details of the way people enter the room, play with their hands, move their chairs or their bodies, for example.

Interpretations as a Means of Reducing Anxiety

Klein's whole approach to analysis was distinctive. She discovered early on that attempts to put patients at ease tended to be counter-productive, with children as well as with adults. The most effective way to build up trust and reduce anxieties was to interpret the patients' material.

The following extract taken from Klein's first book, *The Psychoanalysis of Children* (Klein, 1975, vol. II) demonstrates how this worked in practice. Klein interpreted directly the anxiety which she thought was disturbing the child: she did not attempt to protect the child from her insight but knew that it would bring relief.

> Trude . . . came to me for a single session when she was three years and nine months old, and then had to have her treatment postponed owing to external circumstances. This child was very neurotic and unusually strongly fixated on her mother. She came into my room unwillingly and full of anxiety, and I was obliged to analyse her in a low voice with the door open. But soon she had given me an idea of the nature of her complexes. She insisted upon the flowers in a vase being removed; she threw a little toy man out of a cart into which she had previously put him and heaped abuse on him; she wanted a certain man with a high hat that figured in a picture-book she had brought with her to be taken out of it; and she declared that the cushions in the room had been thrown into disorder by a dog. My immediate interpretation of these utterances in the sense that she desired to do away with her father's penis because it was playing havoc with her mother (as represented by the vase, the cart, the picture-book and the cushion) at once diminished her anxiety and she left me in a much more trustful mood than she had come, and said at home that she would like to come to me again. When, six months later, I was able to resume this little girl's analysis again, it appeared that she had remembered details of her single hour of analysis and that my interpretations had effected a certain amount of positive transference, or rather, some lessening of the negative transference in her. (Klein, 1975, II: 21–2)

Reading such a description the reader may be astonished at the audacity of Klein's interpretations: it probably did not occur to the reader that the vase, the cart, the picture-book and cushion all represented the child's mother or the contents of her body thrown into disorder. Nor may it be immediately obvious why or that they should. What is astonishing is that it obviously did make some kind of sense to the child. It seems in the cold light of day that this kind of interpretation would be more likely to make the child run from a mad-woman; in fact, she stayed and she wanted to come back. We shall be looking at the content of Klein's interpretations later.

This extract also illustrates how one session had an effect on a child which was remembered months later. Klein did not recommend working in this way: she thought that anything other than daily sessions demanded too much of the patient. Their deepest anxieties could not be brought out and held sufficiently; in the case of people suffering from psychoses it could be risky. She objected to the use of the word analysis for therapy taking place less than five times a week. However, Klein clearly did find in practice that even one session can reduce anxieties, and therapists and counsellors today sometimes use this fact.

Klein's Use of Explicit Language

Klein was certain that children's anxieties centred around parts of their parent's bodies, endowed with life and meaning by the child's phantasy. In order to talk about these, she used as far as possible the child's own language. Establishing with parents in advance the child's own words for parts of the body and bodily functions ensured that they knew how she would be speaking to the child. Some of the difficulties involved are illustrated in her description of work with Richard, the 10-year-old described in the *Narrative of a Child Analysis* (Klein, 1975, vol. IV).

> I had asked Richard's mother about the expression he used for his genital and was told that he had none for it and never referred to it. He seemed to have no name for urination and defaecation either; when I introduced the words 'big job' and 'little job' and sometime later 'faeces', he had no difficulty in understanding these expressions.

With adults, Klein also seems to have used expressions such as 'the breast' to refer to certain phantasies. The issue is complicated by the fact that in her writing Klein used different words from those she used with the patient: with the patient she established concepts which had meaning for them from their own material. We shall see later, for example, that she referred to her patient Richard's 'light-blue mummy' which she might have referred to in writing as 'the good breast'.

Free Expression of Fantasies

Klein was prepared to allow her child patients to express their fantasies and fears in a relatively uncontrolled way; as a result they felt free enough to show in considerable detail some very aggressive and passionate fantasies. She described what happened when Trude came back.

> Trude, at the age of four and a quarter, constantly played in the

analytic hour that it was night. We both had to go to sleep. Then she came out of the particular corner which she called her room, stole up to me and made all sorts of threats. She would stab me in the throat, throw me into the courtyard, burn me up, or give me to the policeman. She tried to tie my hands and feet, she lifted the sofa-cover and said she was making 'po-kaki-kucki' (popo = buttocks; kaki = faeces. Kucki, Kucken = look). It turned out that she was looking into the mother's 'popo' for the kakis, which to her represented children. Another time she wanted to hit me on the stomach and declared that she was taking out the 'a-as' (faeces) and making me poor. She then pulled down the cushions, which she repeatedly called 'children', and hid herself with them in the corner of the sofa, where she crouched down with vehement signs of fear, covered herself up, sucked her thumb and wetted herself. This situation always followed her attacks on me.

Here we can see why Klein felt that aggression, sadism and, above all, guilt were important in children. Trude was obviously frightened when she made attacks on Klein in the present and her mother in the past. The setting Klein provided allowed her to show the detail of the attacks she was making. Klein could interpret them to her, enabling the child gradually to bring them under conscious control. The interpretation itself functions to contain the anxiety to some extent: if the analyst can speak it, the anxiety loses some terror for the child.

With adults, too, expression of fantasies can be facilitated in therapy. Lack of restriction on what is said and felt is combined with firm holding of safe boundaries. These reduce the fear of powerfully loving or aggressive feelings spilling over into action. If the therapist is firmly in control the patient can 'let go' more. If the therapist can recognise unwanted feelings and ideas, the patient may be able to too.

Evidence from the Past

Klein's work provided her with material which gave insight into the child's past as well as the present and she used this with her patients, helping them to integrate their earlier selves. Klein continues describing Trude:

Her attitude was, however, similar to that which, at the age of not quite two, she had adopted in bed when she began to suffer from intense *pavor nocturnus* [night fears]. At that time too, she used repeatedly to run into her parents' bedroom in the night without being able to tell them what she wanted. When her sister was born she was two years old and analysis succeeded in revealing what was in her mind at the time and also what were the causes of her anxiety and of her wetting and dirtying her bed. Analysis also succeeded in getting rid of these symptoms.

At this time she had already wished to rob her mother, who was pregnant, of her children, to kill her and to take her place in coitus with the father. These tendencies to hate and aggression were the cause of her fixation to her mother (which at the age of two years was becoming particularly strong), as well as of her feelings of anxiety and guilt. At the time when these phenomena were so prominent in Trude's analysis, she managed to hurt herself almost always just before the analytic hour. I found out that the objects against which she hurt herself (tables, cupboards, stoves, etc.) signified to her (in accordance with the primitive infantile identification) her mother, or at times her father, who was punishing her. In general I have found, especially in very young children, that constantly 'being in the wars' and falling and hurting themselves is closely connected with the castration complex and the sense of guilt. (Klein, 1975, I: 131)

Interpretation of Behaviour and Words

Klein did not simply use play as a means of understanding children: as this work with Trude shows, she interpreted the unconscious meaning of 'ordinary' behaviour outside the consulting room as well. The children also talked: telling stories, relating events, describing dreams or bringing school work. At all times her intention with both adults and children was to make unconscious impulses and fantasies conscious, where they could be tested against other impulses and fantasies and against reality.

Richard was 10 when he came to see Melanie Klein. In *The Narrative of a Child Analysis* it is clear that his difficulties were quite similar to Trude's. He too was strongly fixated on his mother, unable to leave her alone to the extent that he refused to go to school. He too was worried about what his father's penis was doing to his mother. Not all of Klein's patients began with the same anxiety, but these two children show the contrast between the way Klein approached a child of nearly 4 who expressed herself in actions, and a child of 10 who was very conscious of his difficulties and was inhibited in his activities. During the analysis he increasingly used play, drawings and behaviour to show Klein his state of mind, but in this first session he just wanted to talk.

We see Klein going straight to the point, introducing herself by suggesting that Richard knew why he was coming to see her. This was enough to start Richard talking. She listened intently, limiting herself for a long time to exploring his thoughts and worries. Klein refers to herself in the third person.

Mrs K had prepared some little toys and a writing-pad, pencils and chalks on the table, with two chairs by it. When she sat down, Richard also sat down, paying no attention to the toys and looking at her in an expectant and eager way, obviously waiting for her to say something. She suggested that he knew why he was coming to her: he had some difficulties with which he wanted to be helped.

Richard agreed and at once began to talk about his worries. He was afraid of boys he met in the street and of going out by himself, and this fear had been getting worse and worse. It had made him hate school. He also thought much about the war. Of course he knew the Allies were going to win and was not worried, but was it not awful what Hitler did to people, particularly the terrible things he did to the Poles? Did he mean to do the same over here? But he, Richard, felt confident that Hitler would be beaten. (When speaking about Hitler, he went to have a look at a large map hanging on the wall . . .) Mrs K was Austrian, wasn't she? Hitler had been awful to the Austrians though he was Austrian himself . . . Richard also told of a bomb that had fallen near their garden at their old home . . . Poor Cook had been in the house all by herself. He gave a dramatic description of what had happened. The actual damage had not been great; only some windows were blown in and the greenhouse in the garden collapsed. Poor Cook must have been terrified; she went to neighbours to sleep. Richard thought the canaries in their cages must have been shaken and very frightened . . . He again spoke of Hitler's cruel treatment of conquered countries . . . After that he tried to remember whether he had any worries he had not yet mentioned. Oh yes, he often wondered what he was like inside and what other people's insides were like. He was puzzled about the way blood flowed. If one stood for a long time on one's head and all the blood went down into it wouldn't one die?

Mrs K asked whether he also worried about his mother sometimes. [Klein adds a note here that his mother had told her that he was very worried when anything was wrong with her. 'Such information cannot be used often and should become part of interpretations only if it fits very closely into the material. It is safer to rely only on the material given by the child, because otherwise his suspicion might be aroused that the analyst is in close touch with the parents. But in this case I felt the boy was exceptionally ready to talk about all his worries.']

Richard said that he often felt frightened at night, and until four or five years ago he used to be actually terrified. Lately, too, he often felt 'lonely and deserted' before going to sleep. He was frequently worried about Mummy's health: she was sometimes not well. Once she had been brought home on a stretcher after an accident: she had been run over. This had happened before he was born; he had only been told about it, but he often thought about it . . . In the evenings he often feared that a nasty man – a kind of tramp – would come and kidnap Mummy during the night. He then pictured how he, Richard, would go to her help, would scald the tramp with hot water and make him unconscious; and if he, Richard, were to be killed, he would not mind – no, he would mind very much – but this would not stop him from going to Mummy's rescue.

Mrs K asked how he thought the tramp would get into Mummy's room.

Richard said (after some resistance) that he might get in through the window: perhaps he would break in.

Mrs K asked if he also wondered whether the tramp would hurt Mummy.

Richard (reluctantly) answered that he thought the man might hurt her, but he, Richard, would go to her rescue.

Mrs K suggested that the tramp who would hurt Mummy at night seemed to him very much like Hitler who frightened Cook in the air-raid and ill-treated the Austrians. Richard knew that Mrs K was Austrian, and so she too would be ill-treated. At night he might have been afraid that when his parents went to bed something could happen between them with their genitals that would injure Mummy.

At this point, well into the session, Klein has given her first interpretation. We shall discuss the nature of this interpretation. Richard was not immediately as obviously relieved at this point as Trude was. The use of explicit language was perhaps shocking to him in a way it was not to Trude.

Richard looked surprised and frightened. He did not seem to understand what the word 'genital' meant. Up to this point he had obviously understood and had listened with mixed feelings.

Mrs K asked whether he knew what she meant by 'genital'.

Richard first said no, then admitted that he thought he knew. Mummy had told him that babies grew inside her, that she had little eggs there and Daddy put some kind of fluid into her which made them grow. (Consciously he seemed to have no conception of sexual intercourse, nor a name for genitals.) He went on to say that Daddy was very nice, very kind, he wouldn't do anything to Mummy.

Here Klein interprets an aspect of the Oedipus complex. She uses the symbols Richard has given her and shows him how he might have unconscious ideas and thoughts he does not want and which conflict with his more acceptable thoughts and ideas. She does not simply interpret his fear of his father's aggression towards his mother but acknowledges his conscious feelings towards his father too.

Mrs K interpreted that he might have contradictory thoughts about Daddy. Although Richard knew that Daddy was a kind man, at night, when he was frightened, he might fear that Daddy was doing some harm to Mummy. When he thought of the tramp, he did not remember that Daddy, who was in the bedroom with Mummy, would protect her; and that was, Mrs K suggested, because he felt that it was Daddy himself who might hurt Mummy. (At that moment Richard looked impressed and evidently accepted the interpretation.) In day-time he thought Daddy was nice, but at night when he, Richard, could not see his parents and did not know what they were doing in bed, he might have felt that Daddy was bad and dangerous and all the terrible things which happened to Cook, and the shaking and breaking of windows, were happening to Mummy . . . Such thoughts might be in his mind though he was not at all aware of them. Just now he had spoken of the terrible things the Austrian Hitler did to the Austrians. By this he meant that Hitler was in a way ill-treating his own people, including Mrs K, just as the bad Daddy would ill-treat Mummy.

Richard, though he did not say so, appeared to accept this interpretation. From the beginning of the session he seemed extremely keen to tell all about himself, as if he had been waiting for this chance for a long time. Though he repeatedly showed anxiety and surprise and rejected some of the interpretations, his whole attitude towards the end of the hour had altered and he was less tense. He said he had noticed the toys, the pad and the pencils on the table, but he did not like toys, he liked talking and thinking. He was very friendly and satisfied when he left Mrs K and said he was glad to come again the next day. (Klein, 1975, IV: 19)

Although Richard had not liked all of what Mrs Klein had told him, he clearly appreciated her efforts.

Interpreting the Transference

Klein's first interpretation to Richard in this session was a transference interpretation: it focused on Richard's relation with the analyst, linking it to his relations with his parents. It drew together Richard's expressed anxieties about Hitler with his unconscious anxieties about Klein and about what went on at night between his parents. Klein believed in general that 'there should be no session without a transference interpretation' (Klein, 1975, IV: 22 *n*. ii). In these interpretations she traced the patient's emotions towards the analyst, always referring them back to the original objects. This was a major innovation and one which not all analysts follow.

In Richard's material we can see that his anxieties about Klein and her relation to Hitler emerged very early on and were followed by talking about the bomb: by giving an interpretation linking his feelings about Klein with his fears about his parents' sexual intercourse, Klein was staying very close to his expressed anxieties.

Although Klein thought it was important to interpret the transference, she did not always do so immediately.

When the patient is deeply engrossed with his relation with his father or mother, brother or sister, with his experiences in the past or even in the present, it is necessary to give him every opportunity to enlarge on these subjects. The reference to the analyst then has to come later. On other occasions the analyst might feel that, whatever the patient is speaking about, the whole emotional emphasis lies on his relation to the analyst. In this case, the interpretations would first refer to the transference. (Klein, 1975, IV: 19)

Emphasis on the importance of transference interpretations is one of the distinctive features of the Kleinian approach. Chapter 5 takes this up in more detail.

Working with the Oedipus Complex

We can see in the sessions with both Richard and Trude that Klein interpreted the Oedipus complex as a priority. She picked up the rivalry, jealousy and aggressiveness that the child felt towards his or her parents, as well as love towards them and the desire to make babies with each of them.

As Steiner (1985) has pointed out, in the Oedipus myth Oedipus puts out his eyes not only to punish himself but also not to see what he has done. As is clear from the quoted extracts, Klein's analysis of the Oedipus conflict included helping her patients to see feelings they did not want to know they had. In Richard's second session, for example, Richard told Klein that his mother's accident had in fact taken place when he was 2; Klein suggested that he might have thought it was before he was born because he wanted to convince himself that it was nothing to do with himself. Her suggestion in this second session that Richard might have jealous and angry feelings towards his parents and lie to himself about them (he had said Ribbentrop lied about Britain being the aggressor) brought after a moment a smile of relief.

Since Klein was clear that there was a distinction between the child's phantasies of its parents and the real parents, she was not afraid of uncovering the roots of the child's hostility towards either herself or the parents. Kleinian therapy is unlikely to encourage adult patients to attack their parents: clearer insight into their faults goes hand in hand with insight into the patient's own.

Erna at 6, for example, was convinced that her mother's total preoccupation was with spoiling and damaging Erna's pleasure in life: all the things she did and all the pleasure she took herself were simply to make Erna suffer envy and jealousy. Klein often described real abuse of children, but these phantasies arose from Erna's own sadism and were quite unrealistic. Even where she had to deal with actual conscious or unconscious hostility from the parents to the child, Klein was able to work with the child's interpretations of events which had invariably added a further dimension to the negative relations.

> Of course it is possible that, if the child has to associate with people lacking in insight, neurotic, or otherwise harmful to him, the result may be that we cannot completely clear up his own neurosis or that it may be evoked again by his surroundings. According to my experience,

however, we can even in these cases do much to mitigate matters and to induce a better development . . . Even in such cases I have found that the children were enabled by analysis . . . better to stand the test of an unfavourable milieu and to suffer less than before being analysed. And I have proved repeatedly that when a child becomes less neurotic it becomes less tiresome to those around it who are themselves neurotic or lacking in insight, and in this way too analysis will exercise only a favourable influence on their relationships. (Klein, 1975, I: 165)

Interpreting the Negative Transference

Klein interpreted hatred and rivalry in connection with herself as well as in connection with the parents both in child and adult patients. In her paper for the Symposium on Child Analysis in 1927 (Klein, 1975, vol. I), Klein criticised Anna Freud for refusing to work with the negative transference in this way. She suggested that by attracting all the child's positive feelings Anna Freud in fact would be making life more difficult for the child's parents, who would be left with all the child's negative feelings. She herself worked the other way round, analysing all the child's feelings and phantasies towards herself, both negative and positive, thereby helping the child towards a better appreciation of the full reality of his or her impulses and feelings. By drawing out the child's hostile feelings towards herself, standing for the parents, she could work with these feelings with the child and allow the actual parents the benefit of the child's more positive feelings which gradually surfaced through the analysis. With adult patients, the beneficiary of this process can be a husband or wife, for example.

Klein said she did not have complaints from parents about the children's behaviour, but that the first effect of the analysis was an improvement in the child's relation with the parents and others around them. Conscious understanding followed this improvement. Once, she said, with Erna, anal-sadistic impulses were emerging with considerable force and Erna was acting upon them in the outside world. Her conclusion was that she had not sufficiently analysed the negative transference: the child's negative feelings towards her, the analyst. The results confirmed this belief.

Internal Parents

Klein never attempted to work with children and their actual parents: she found it sufficient to work with their relationship with their parents in analysis with her. Her belief in the importance of unconscious phantasies of parents never wavered, with considerable consequences for the practice of child analysis. Analysis of children's relations with their internal phantasy mothers changed their relationship with their real mothers.

Erna, for example, tore up and wetted pieces of paper which she said were variously babies, her father's penis, her mother's breast and faeces; and then ate them. Here Klein interpreted the child's attacks on these objects and her taking them inside her chewed up and destroyed.

Erna was a very disturbed child with passionate and terrifying fantasies towards her mother. Her relation with her internal mother at first was part of a system in which she lived in a fantasy-world of her own making, with as little contact as possible with the real world. It took some time before Klein could convince her that she was in fact terrified of her mother. Eventually Klein was able to put Erna in touch with the origins of this terror in her own sadism towards her mother. 'At this point, after having represented her ideas of persecution in play, Erna would often say with astonishment: "But Mother can't really have meant to do that? She's very fond of me *really*."' When she first came to analysis Erna never criticised her mother. 'As her contact with reality improved and her unconscious hatred of her mother became more conscious, she began to criticise her as a real person with ever greater frankness and at the same time her relations with her improved' (Klein, 1975, II: 47).

The Interpretation of a Real-life Event

A later session with Richard (no. 61) shows, among other things, how Klein interpreted material arising from a real-life event. In this session we also see Klein expressing sympathy for Richard: her 'interpretation only' rule was sometimes broken and she does not criticise herself for this here. Richard reported that:

> early in the morning he had found his father lying on the floor, ill and nearly fainting. He had called mummy, who 'burst into the room' followed by Paul (his brother); they carried his father to the bedroom and put him to bed. He made this report dramatically, enjoyed the part he had played and his being able to relate such an important event, but at the same time he was clearly very upset. He added that he hoped his father would recover. The detailed description of how his father was being nursed showed that in his mind his father had turned into a baby and Richard into an adult who would look after the baby.

At this point Klein adds a note: 'Previous material had shown that by reversing the father–son relation Richard could combat his jealousy and maintain feelings of love and compassion towards his father.' She notes later that this is the only point at which Richard appeared sad: during the rest of the session he seemed persecuted, though by the time he parted from her he had become 'serious and sad'.

To return to the session, Klein continues 'He asked Mrs K what she thought about all this, and was pleased when she expressed her sympathy.' He then added more details about what had happened.

After he had told Mrs K all these details a great change took place in Richard. He had been quite emotional, though fairly composed, and his face had been expressive and lively. Now he became restless, turned pale, and looked anxious and persecuted. He tried to explore the packages which had been left in the playroom the previous day, and kicked the [tent] poles . . . He returned to the table and again spoke about his father's illness and repeated that it was a good thing that his father need not be operated on. He took a penknife out of his pocket, saying it was his own and he need not borrow Mrs K's this time, opened it, and started scratching the poles with it. Then, standing at the window and turning his back on Mrs K, he hit his teeth with the knife.

Mrs K interpreted that the previous day [in his session] he had operated on and killed a moth which stood for his father; and when he had just now tried to cut the poles with his knife, this expressed his fear that he had attacked his father. When his father actually became ill, this had made Richard feel he was the cause of it. Because he felt guilty and wanted to punish himself, he had turned the knife against himself and hit his teeth.

Richard had become less restless during this interpretation and the colour returned to his face. He looked impressed and understanding. (It appeared to me that this insight must have been almost conscious.) But soon he became very aggressive with his knife. He slashed at the wooden poles, scratched along the window-pane, attempted to cut the table and nearly cut open the packages. Mrs K told him that he should not do that. Richard also repeatedly put the blade in his own mouth. Mrs K warned him that he might hurt himself and he stopped it. Then he walked about with the open knife pointing directly at himself so that if he had slipped he would have hurt himself. Mrs K warned him again and Richard closed the knife.

Mrs K interpreted that he felt that the injured, cut-up dead moth-father was inside him; this feeling was increased by his father's illness and the fear of his death. Richard wanted to remove this ill, dangerous or dead father out of his inside and therefore turned the knife on himself, which would imply hurting or even killing himself. The pole, which stood for daddy's big genital, was also felt to be inside him and to be attacked there. Richard's attempt to smash the table and his cutting at the window meant the same thing. He felt very guilty about such aggressive wishes and wanted to punish himself.

Richard looked very frightened and miserable and said he wished he were 'not here' . . . *Mrs K* interpreted that she had changed into the injured mummy containing the injured and therefore dangerous daddy. Richard felt so guilty that he attempted to blame Mrs K, representing also the bad mummy, for daddy's illness.

Richard then explored the playroom and began first to attack it (for example, taking out some soot and hitting the draining board and a stove-pipe with an axe), saying that if it were his house he would smash up the whole thing. Klein interpreted further his fear of the enormous destroyed father-genital which had to be smashed and got rid of. After some more interpretations, Richard began to try to get his hand inside one of the packages and then to clear up the building, including taking soot from the stove and cleaning the lavatory. During this rather hectic activity Richard had asked only a few things, the last being whether there had been any raids by the RAF. Klein interpreted that

> Richard had now attempted another way of dealing with his fear. If he could clear Mrs K's, Mummy's and his own inside of the dangerous 'big job' which was in his mind the same now as the beetle, the moth and the dangerous genital of his father, then he might make everybody all right again. This implied that he also wished to rid his father's inside of what had made him ill, and this meant that Richard's 'big job', which had so often represented bombs in his mind, might have contributed to his father's illness. (Klein, 1975, IV: 301–3)

Klein included material from the child's daily life in her analysis of children. She was very clear, and made it clear to the child, that the child wove experiences into existing phantasies and interpreted events in the light of present anxieties. Richard's anxieties about his father had lasted for many years: his father's illness brought a new fear that made them appear more real. Richard's response was to attack; first himself, then the room, and in phantasy Mrs Klein and his mother. Klein permitted the attack while keeping it within limits of safety, and showed him how it linked with his fears. This gradually enabled him to begin to try to make amends.

It is also evident that Richard's relief at Klein's interpretations was followed by more and different anxieties emerging. These in turn were analysed and relief obtained. Each anxiety seemed to originate from a deeper, earlier level. His first symbolisation of his father was of him as a baby and Richard as a man but this did not last. It was followed by fears about his attacks on his father in which his father was represented by a moth he had killed: this in turn was followed by attacks on the tent poles and fears about smashing his mother. The tent poles were a more inanimate and therefore more primitive symbol for his father or his penis than the baby or the moth. His mother at this point was represented by the whole building: Richard with this was symbolising a mother he and his father could get inside and which was enormous by comparison with himself, representing a phantasy of a mother/breast arising from a very early age indeed.

Reading this session it is clear that Klein may have felt quite anxious herself, watching Richard becoming more persecuted and more violent. By containing her anxieties and simply interpreting his she gave him permission to show her the extent of his destructive reaction to his father's illness. The temptation to calm him down, perhaps by stopping the analysis or perhaps in some other way must have been great. Because she did not do this, Klein uncovered very primitive anxieties and phantasies about his mother behind Richard's fears about his father. Once uncovered and acknowledged they could be tested against reality and lose some of their frightening qualities.

The Setting

Klein discovered with children that a firm and regular setting was very important. Close attention paid to unconscious messages from patients, young or old, made it clear that changes of time or place or changes in the analyst were picked up and fed into their unconscious phantasies of the situation. Some patients were very sensitive to the slightest change in the setting. Changes of time, in particular, tended to be interpreted in terms of the power relations between patient and analyst; it could make patients quite anxious to have their requests for a change met too easily if they then interpreted the analyst as too weak to withstand their demands, or as too keen to placate the patient out of fear or because they had been seduced by the patient. Klein learnt to interpret such requests and found that sometimes (though not always) it was more supportive to the patient to refuse them and to analyse the consequences.

In order to establish the role of the patient's phantasies in the way they interpreted the world and the people in it, Klein also found it useful to keep the amount of information patients had about the analyst to the bare minimum. In this way it was clearer for both patient and analyst that it was the patient's phantasies which led them to make assumptions about the analyst. These assumptions could reveal much about the patient's inner world.

Klein was very clear that the role of the analyst was to provide understanding and interpretation. Properly used, these give the warm holding which is needed to enable deep anxieties to be exposed, contained and modified. Any other kind of gratification was a confusion at best and at times could be experienced as an abuse. She was upset when Ferenczi and some other analysts later turned to practices which included considerable physical contact with patients: she felt that they had abandoned analysis. She warned her own students that Freud had said: 'If the first generation hold hands with their patients, the next generation will take them to bed.'

Working with Psychosis

Klein's paper 'The Importance of Symbol Formation in the Development of the Ego' was written in 1930. In this paper she describes the analysis of a small boy she called Dick, who at the age of 4 'as regards the poverty of his vocabulary and of his intellectual attainments, was on the level of a child of about fifteen or eighteen months. Adaptation to reality and emotional relations to his environment were almost entirely lacking. This child, Dick . . . was indifferent to the presence or absence of his mother or nurse . . . He had almost no interests, did not play, and had no contact with his environment . . . .' (Klein, 1975, I: 221)

With Dick, Klein felt she had at first to interpret more on the basis of her own experience than she would have liked. We also see her giving the child reassuring information. Later analysts (e.g. Tustin, 1974) have commented on the enormous emotional pressure on adults exerted by psychotic anxieties in children.

Klein describes the first session she had with Dick:

> The first time Dick came to me . . . he manifested no sort of affect [i.e. emotion] when his nurse handed him over to me. When I showed him the toys I had put ready, he looked at them without the faintest interest. I took a big train and put it beside a smaller one and called them 'Daddy-train' and 'Dick-train'. Thereupon he picked up the train I called 'Dick' and made it roll to the window and said 'Station'. I explained: 'The station is mummy; Dick is going into mummy.' He left the train, ran into the space between the outer and inner doors of the room, shut himself in, saying 'dark' and ran out again directly. He went through this performance several times. I explained to him: 'It is dark inside mummy. Dick is inside dark mummy.' Meantime he picked up the train again, but soon ran back into the space between the doors. While I was saying that he was going into dark mummy, he said twice in a questioning way: 'Nurse?' I answered: 'Nurse is soon coming', and this he repeated and used the words later quite correctly, retaining them in his mind. (Klein, 1975, I: 225)

Dick's development in the first week was striking. By the end of the third session he was looking at the toys and greeting his nurse with unusual delight when she arrived for him, and at the fourth session he actually cried when his nurse left him. Klein had tried to do nothing other than to analyse him as far as possible in her usual fashion.

This work was truly revolutionary. Freud and other analysts had believed it was impossible to analyse people suffering from psychoses: they felt that the lack of emotional contact would make analysis impossible. Klein demonstrated that this lack of contact could be overcome by sufficient understanding on the part of the analyst. She found that there was a healthy and sane part of the personality which could make contact with the analyst.

Klein analysed only one adult suffering from a psychosis, briefly. She worked from home and had only a housekeeper: she felt that this was insufficient to enable both her and the patient to feel safe enough to allow exploration of a pyschosis. However, she encouraged her students to take up this work.

The Analysis of Envy

Klein's technique developed with experience. As she understood more and saw more, she interpreted certain difficulties sooner. Writing in the *Narrative of a Child Analysis* she said that, looking back, she would have interpreted Richard's envy of her sooner and more clearly if she had recognised it then.

The analysis of envy can produce quite dramatic results. Where it can be recognised and overcome, past good experiences can be remembered and love regained: this can create a benevolent circle in which many good feelings which previously had to be denied can now be tolerated. Uncovering envy brings the possibility of discovering pleasures given and received which have never been acknowledged but instead forgotten, devalued or destroyed in some other way. Analysis of envy brings the possibility of recovering a sense not only of loved and loving internal parents, but also a loved and loving self which has been attacked, destroyed and so lost: this in turn allows other anxieties to be borne where previously they were felt to be too dangerous.

Klein's sympathy for the patient was vital in allowing her to interpret envy in a way which made knowledge of it bearable. She had an ability to convey her understanding and warm acceptance of the patient's distress at his or her own destructiveness, while remaining adamant that it *was* destructive and that the patient had some choice about whether to continue in this way or not.

Conclusion

Klein's idea of analysis was illuminated by her observations on children: her awareness of the deep conflict between different impulses enabled her to work alongside the more sane and life-supporting aspects of her patients in their struggle with the more destructive aspects of themselves. Her recognition of unconscious guilt about the damaging aspects of the defences of splitting and denial and her conviction of the importance of unconscious processes kept her analysing deeper and deeper anxieties as the patient made them clear to her. She could see the reduction in fear and anxiety and the increase in inner strength which accompanied recognition and acceptance of distasteful but true feelings. Her understanding of these in herself, partly a result of continuing self-analysis which she carried on all her life, helped her to approach her patients with deep sympathy.

4

Criticisms and Rebuttals

Some of the criticisms levelled at Klein and Kleinian therapists are directed at all analysts: others are specific to Kleinians and their ideas within the analytical or therapeutic community. The criticisms can be divided into those directed at the behaviour of the therapist and those directed at theoretical formulations. There are also political challenges to Klein and to analysis itself. Klein herself was quite critical of others, and her own position was established partly through disagreement with others. This chapter also includes criticisms Klein made of the ways other analysts worked.

It is difficult to show readers how and why Kleinians think all that they do. There is really no substitute for reading detailed reports of analyses and for being analysed oneself. Many of the criticisms and rebuttals are between analysts who have access to patients and may have some possibility of observing whether each other's insights help them or not. But the way a therapist of any kind works depends on his or her personality and emotional availability as well as his or her training, so some observations may be very hard for certain people to make even if they are analysts. For those outside this small group of people, any real attempt to check Kleinian insights is extremely difficult. It is not sufficient to say, for example, 'I don't remember hating my mother or being afraid of my own aggression or wanting to have sex with my mother and kill my father.' In the theory one is not supposed to remember these things.

There is little point in trying too hard to convince anyone of the validity of Kleinian ideas. People have to try them out for themselves in their own lives. Many people read Klein and find revelations about themselves and their families. Some people feel an instant affinity with Kleinian ideas: others do not. Some risk trying Kleinian ideas in their work or their relationships and find them useful; they may then take the risk again, perhaps seeking a Kleinian supervisor or therapist for themselves. Others are simply not interested: some even experience a revulsion against some of the ideas and cannot bear to read further; this reaction is not, however, unique to Kleinian writings but can be experienced towards those of other therapists.

Kleinian ideas can, however, make sense in a way which others do not. Over a period of twenty years I have made many observations which have gradually convinced me of parts of psycho-analytical theory which initially I rejected. It was not until I read my son a New Guinean folk story that I was really convinced that the Oedipus complex existed. In the story a mother carrying her baby son ran away from her husband. While he chased her a rock fell on him and killed him, whereupon my son looked up with a delighted expression and exclaimed '– so then she could marry her son!' Without such direct evidence many of Klein's ideas, like Freud's, are incredible.

The Risks of Child Analysis

Klein was under attack from the very beginning for her methods of analysing children. At a symposium on child analysis in 1927 she took up the misgivings of analysts: we can deduce from her discussion some of the accusations being made against her and against Freud himself when he undertook the analysis of a child. The issue of safety and the risks involved was paramount: this was not simply a result of Hug-Hellmuth's murder but had obviously arisen before, since Hug-Hellmuth herself warned against analysis for children touching their deepest feelings. Some child psycho-therapists today speak in similar terms, suggesting that it is dangerous to uncover too many of children's negative and aggressive feelings towards their parents.

Klein began her paper by emphasising the importance of Freud's analysis (through the boy's father) of Hans, aged 5: 'not only did it show the presence and evolution of the Oedipus complex in children and demonstrate the forms in which it operates in them; it showed also that these unconscious tendencies could safely and most profitably be brought into consciousness.' She goes on to quote Freud:

> But I must now inquire what harm was done to Hans by dragging to light in him complexes such as are not only repressed by children but dreaded by their parents. Did the little boy proceed to take some serious action as regards what he wanted from his mother? or did his evil intentions against his father give place to evil deeds? Such misgivings will no doubt have occurred to many doctors, who misunderstand the nature of psychoanalysis and think that wicked instincts are strengthened by being made conscious. . . .
>
> On the contrary, the only results of the analysis were that Hans

recovered, that he ceased to be afraid of horses, and that he got on to rather familiar terms with his father. . . (Klein, 1975, I: 139–40)

Both Anna Freud and Hermine Hug-Hellmuth were loath to touch the more aggressive and sexual phantasies children had against their parents. They were not only afraid of alienating parents by exposing to children their aggression towards their parents, but they also wanted the children to have good and friendly feelings towards themselves, thinking that this was necessary for the children to be able to work with them.

Klein had withstood hearing her own son talk of wanting to kill his father and make babies with his mother: she had helped her small patients to talk about their desires to do quite horrifying things to their parents, and the results had been a reduction in the children's anxieties, a blossoming of their intellectual interests and curiosity and a noticeable improvement in the relation of the children with their parents.

As a result of her experience, Klein was certain that aggressive phantasies were far less dangerous when analysed than when left alone. She had found that the child's aggressiveness was matched and in constant conflict with powerful loving and reparative drives: in order to help the child with this conflict, acknowledgement of the aggression was essential.

Even in Dick, the psychotic boy, Klein found not only cruel sadism but also enormous empathy and capacity to love, which she felt his mother had overlooked. Since the aggression was aimed at a distorted version of the parents, bringing it into the open enabled a more realistic view of the parents to develop, causing the aggressiveness to be modified. In the process the ego was strengthened by enabling it to take back and own the hated parts of itself which were attributed to the hated parents. This process, she believed, could only bring benefit to the child and to those around.

Behaviour of the Therapist

'Kleinian Analysts Do Not Behave like Human Beings'
This criticism and its rebuttal comprise several parts. Some of the issues as they relate to present-day practice are discussed further in Chapter 5.

Paula Heimann in her paper 'On Countertransference' (1950), discussing the feelings of analysts for their patients, described Ferenczi's view, 'which not only acknowledges that the analyst has a wide variety of feelings towards his patient, but recommends that he should at times express them openly'. Alice Balint (1936) had suggested that 'such honesty on the part of the analyst is helpful and in keeping with the respect for the truth inherent in psycho-analysis.' Other analysts too, Heimann wrote, 'have claimed that it makes the analyst more "human" when he expresses his feelings to a patient and that it helps him to build up a "human" relationship with him' (Heimann, 1950: 81). Heimann (as well as Klein) was adamant that this was wrong.

Heimann also pointed out how 'Many candidates are afraid and feel guilty when they become aware of feelings towards their patients and consequently aim at avoiding any emotional response and at becoming completely unfeeling and detached.' This led to analysts behaving in a 'coldly distant' way. Heimann makes it clear that this is not the way an analyst should behave either, and this sentiment is very much shared by present-day Kleinians. In my experience, Kleinian therapists of all kinds relate to others in a warm though not intrusive way, both as people and in a professional context. They have a respect for other people as people, though they may disagree strongly and firmly in arguments about theory.

Klein's patients and pupils found her both warm and encouraging. Grosskurth traced one of Klein's child patients, who took the book Grosskurth gave him and kissed the photograph of Klein on the back murmuring 'Dear old Melanie' (Grosskurth, 1986: 374).

Therapists of other persuasions sometimes argue that it is more 'equal' to disclose information about the self. Some therapists or counsellors go to some lengths to assert their equality with their clients. The co-counselling movement, for example, asserts that anyone can be a therapist, and that it is simply a matter of taking it in turns. Other counsellors believe that it is important to tell clients about their own lives, their own successes and failures, in order to establish that they are not 'superior'.

Kleinians do not work like this. They are more concerned to avoid muddying painful issues, such as the fact that the client is paying the therapist for help and presumably thereby acknowledging that the therapist has something the client does not yet have. Giving information about the therapist's real life would add to difficulties in disentangling the client's fantasies from reality and distract from the task in hand.

Kleinians see part of their task as helping the client to cope with unequal relationships in which differences can be tolerated without being exaggerated. Differences in terms of what one has and the other has not are fundamental to our existence and our development. If we could not tolerate the fact that the breast had milk which we wanted and did not have we may not have been able to tolerate the fact that teachers had information we needed, that other people have capacities we do not and that the opposite sex has genitals and a capacity to give us babies which we do not have alone. Coping with the frustrations of our dependence on others to provide us with things we need is essential if we are to learn, to work creatively and to have babies.

The therapist's abilities to give to the client need also to be seen in context. Klein pointed out that if a therapist pays attention to an idealisation of them by a client (for example, as having 'everything' when the client has 'nothing') they will soon discover that the client at the same time sees the therapist quite differently. Behind an idealisation of the therapist may be a view of the therapist as having nothing, being at best quite useless and unable to help even themselves, let alone the client; at worst both threatening and damaging the client and making things even worse for them. Real-life information would confuse such issues. A therapist who works with the underlying denigration of them by their client is unlikely to remain feeling arrogant and superior for long.

Some analysts and other therapists undoubtedly do behave in an arrogant and superior way, both towards patients and to others: Kleinian analysts, just like anyone else, object to this kind of behaviour and see it as an unfortunate aspect of human nature which could be reduced by a good analysis.

It is also important to distinguish the way someone is in the consulting room from the way they are outside it. Klein herself was sometimes criticised by her enemies for being arrogant, self-opinionated and frightening. She was quite clearly capable of being very sharp with people who disagreed with her. She did not allow her students to make excuses about shoddy work. But Hanna Segal as a patient and colleague of Klein's said that Klein 'had a gift for equality'. Inside the consulting room and when her convictions were not under attack, she seems to have been sympathetic, understanding and very willing to listen to and encourage the ideas of her students.

The transference relation of patient to analyst may give rise to the idea that an analyst is behaving in an inhuman, superior way even when he or she is not: we have all felt our parents to be humiliatingly superior at times. As an analysis progresses, this view of the analyst changes, but some critics of analysis and some therapists themselves have broken off analysis too soon for this process to work itself out.

A client who had been in counselling for two weeks told his counsellor that he had begun counselling his friends. It became clear that this meant telling them what to do in a very high-handed way. The counsellor was distressed to hear her own gentle exploration of the client's difficulties being perceived in this way. She wondered if the client felt she was being high-handed with him and asked him: he said no and was rather surprised that the counsellor had seen him as being anything other than helpful to his friends.

The client was seriously obsessional and had a constant sense of his father behaving in a very dictatorial way towards him. At the beginning of her work with this client the counsellor had felt that her supervisor was looking over her shoulder in accusation. This was a feeling she had never had before and her supervisor had pointed out that it might have been a result of her unconscious response to the patient's psychopathology. The patient seemed indeed to feel a constant sense of being watched and ordered about in a very paralysing and restricting way by his father and it would not have been surprising if he had transferred this to the therapist.

The counsellor watched her own behaviour with this client particularly carefully, but she also tried to help him to see how he seemed to be identifying with a distorted version of the counsellor.

Another strand of the accusation of being 'inhuman' is that Klein-ian analysts are sometimes criticised for being too rigid about times of sessions, for their insistence on not keeping patients or clients waiting and for their emphasis on maintaining consistency in their behaviour, their dress and the setting of the therapy. They have been accused of 'playing power games' and refusing to behave 'like a human being' when they insist on analysing lateness or any request for a change of time, or for refusing to extend sessions when the patient arrives late, for example.

All of these criticisms are contested by Kleinians. Kleinian therapists work from the basis that the relationship with the patient or client is professional and not social. They also work with the patient's unconscious impulses and reactions, not simply with conscious ones. Some of these involve psychotic aspects of the personality. The firmness of the setting and the refusal of the analyst to disclose information about the self both relate to this.

Ordinary social rules do not work well with people who are seriously disturbed. During a psychotic breakdown someone may not, for example, react to normal social hints that it is time to leave; they may ask very intrusive questions or attempt to invade other people's space, while reacting in a very frightened or strange way to other people's attempts to come close. In this situation extreme clarity about boundaries may be not only helpful but essential. In therapy, firm boundaries can enable the psychotic levels of the personality to be explored or held safely: without them the client or patient can be afraid of becoming too entangled with the therapist; of taking the therapist over or being taken over, for example. Boundaries around the patient's time and around the information given to the patient can be vital in these situations.

The firmness of time boundaries can also be reassuring to patients who are testing out their own power and the ability of the therapist to hold them, to resist seduction and to survive attacks on their integrity. Just as a small child is not helped by being allowed too many liberties, so a patient or client is not helped by being allowed to take liberties. The anger at being kept out or kept within clear boundaries (which can be dealt with in the therapy) is preferable to the abuse and potential guilt involved in allowing the child or patient too much access to the parent or therapist.

No Reassurance

Kleinians are sometimes criticised for making no attempt to make their patients comfortable or to indulge in chat at the beginning of therapy. Ferenczi was one of the analysts who wrote that he used other methods such as reassurance with his patients: some other analysts today do this too. Some Middle Group analysts (though by no means all) have at times advocated behaving in ways which go far beyond analysis and interpretation, including encouraging physical contact such as stroking. Klein was very worried about this and objected strongly that this was not analysis.

We have already described how Klein was very clear that the attempt to reassure patients is not helpful. She found that with small children her interpretations not only established the analytical situation but also immediately reduced anxiety in the child. This reduction in anxiety enabled the analysis to take place, and established her as a trustworthy person with whom the child would stay. Far from creating a distance, it was in fact the interpretations which enabled her to come close to the child.

> For instance, when Rita, who was a very ambivalent child, felt a resistance she at once wanted to leave the room, and I had to make an interpretation immediately so as to resolve this resistance. As soon as I had clarified for her the cause of her resistance – always carrying it back to its original object and situation – it was resolved, and she would become friendly and trustful again and continue playing, supplying in its various details a confirmation of the interpretation I had just given. (Klein, 1975, II: 21).

Kleinians believe that reassurance is likely to be interpreted by the patient as a sign of the therapist's difficulty in picking up and taking seriously negative feelings and issues expressed. It is far more important and effective for the therapist to work with whatever seems to give rise to a desire for reassurance.

Klein illustrated in her *Narrative of a Child Analysis* (1975, IV: 320–5) how she felt that reassurance was not helpful. Richard asked her if she had kept an envelope and recycled it as part of 'the war effort'. Klein answered that she had kept it and Richard responded by being pleased and saying that she was 'patriotic'. Immediately he turned against a girl seen out of the window. Klein saw this as his splitting her into a 'patriotic Mrs Klein' and a 'bad girl' outside and felt she could have avoided this if she had taken up his suspicion of her in the first place. Because she did not, Richard had understood that his suspicious self was not admissible in relation with her and had tried to get rid of it outside.

It is not only with children that introductions are kept to a minimum. An adult client probably does not really want to waste their time or money for a pretence at a social relationship; if they do, there may be some kind of attack going on in which the therapist's professional self is to be prevented from working. This needs to be taken up as a matter of urgency since any attack on other people's ability to work or their creativity is likely to cause clients difficulty in their own work or creativity.

Klein and her followers are clear that any modification of the analytical technique, whether out of a desire to appear more 'human' or for any other reason, is depriving the patient of a service which is capable of offering them something unique.

'Kleinian Analysts are Too Active'

Some analysts feel that Kleinians do too much; they should wait and let the patient do the work, not be so ready to speak. Some other analysts will spend a lot more time sitting and waiting for the patient to speak than Kleinians normally do.

Kleinians are unashamedly active, though there are circumstances when they too are silent for long periods. By definition, the patient's deepest and most troublesome anxieties and difficulties are hidden from consciousness; the patient will not come to them alone however long the analyst waits. Klein's own son's failure to ask about the role of the father in intercourse illustrates this.

There is an awareness that this activity on the analyst's part can (and indeed is likely to) arouse the patient's envy of the analyst's understanding and insight. The Kleinian view is that it is very important to expose this envy and work it through, not to avoid it or allow it actually to spoil the work by withholding interpretations. A joke illustrates the differences between two styles of analysis:

> Two patients meet on the way to analysis; the first goes to an Anna Freudian, the second to a Kleinian. The first says to the second, 'What's the hurry? Nothing happens for the first half hour anyway.' The Kleinian patient says 'What do you mean? She'll start without me!'

This joke also draws attention to the way Kleinian analysts pay close attention to the details of lateness and punctuality which can be very revealing. Patients can in fact get very upset over a matter of even two minutes' lateness and may make it very clear (though in a disguised fashion) that this is not an irrelevancy.

'Too Much Emphasis on Aggression and Negative Feelings'

Klein was often accused of being too pessimistic and of placing too much emphasis on negative feelings. Elizabeth Bott Spillius in her book entitled *Melanie Klein Today* (1988) takes up this criticism:

> There had been little focusing on aggression in psychoanalytic theory before the 1920s, even though Freud's case histories give ample illustration of his interpreting rivalry and aggressiveness as well as unconscious sexual wishes. Certainly Klein was very much aware of destructiveness and of the anxiety it arouses, which was one of her earliest areas of research, but she also stressed, both in theory and practice, the importance of love, the patient's concern for his objects, of guilt and of reparation. Further, in her later work especially, she conveys a strong feeling of support to the patient when negative feelings were being uncovered: this is especially clear in *Envy and Gratitude* (1957). It is my impression that she was experienced by her patients not as an adversary but as an ally in their struggles to accept feelings they hated in themselves and were therefore trying to deny and obliterate. I think it is this attitude that gave the feeling of 'balance' that Segal says was so important in her experience of Klein as an analyst (Segal, 1982). Certainly that sort of balance is something that present Kleinian analysts are consciously striving for. (Spillius, 1988, II: 8).

Spillius read all the papers, many of them unpublished, written by Kleinian analysts for membership of the British Psychoanalytical Society, and she gives an account of changes over the years in Kleinian practice:

> There are certain strikingly original exceptions, but most of the papers of the 1950s and 1960s, especially those by young and relatively inexperienced analysts, tend to emphasize the patient's destructiveness in a way that we would now assume might have felt persecuting to the patient . . . Gradually . . . several trends of change emerged in the papers of the 1960s and 1970s . . . destructiveness began to be interpreted in a more balanced way. (Spillius, 1988, II: 7)

Theory

Some aspects of theory affect the behaviour of the therapist more than others. During the Controversial Discussions many criticisms were made of Kleinian ideas; some of these were repeated by Otto F. Kernberg (1969). In this paper Kernberg detailed the criticisms of the ego-psychologists and also listed those of Klein's insights which he believed had subsequently been incorporated by ego-psychologist analysts. A few of the main criticisms of Klein's theory which are of relevance to counselling are detailed below.

'It's Not Scientific'

Psychoanalysis as a whole has often been and continues to be accused of being 'unscientific'. Analysts during the war had to struggle with the British Medical Association for recognition: as a group they were accused of lacking a scientific basis for their work. Glover was the analyst who had to defend psychoanalysis before the British Medical Association: it was he who in turn accused Klein of not being scientific.

Jonathan Miller (1983) also challenges the scientific status of analysis:

> After nearly eighty years psychoanalysis has failed to arrive at anything which one could properly call consensus, and the vehemence with which the various schools disagree with one another has led some of the more uncharitable sceptics to conclude that the Freudian enterprise should be classified as a religious dogma and not as a scientific theory. In which case the contribution made by Melanie Klein must surely be considered as one of its most interesting and influential heresies.

This does not do justice to the way Freud's ideas have changed and developed over time. Shortly after his death it did seem that some of his followers wanted to treat his work as dogma, but there have now been many new developments. Freud changed his opinions and theories many times throughout his life as his observations challenged his formulations. So too have his successors, who include those who owe insight to the work of Melanie Klein.

Klein did not write in the way in which Freud did, constantly building theories and referring to other writers. Her observations, however, were written up in a very detailed fashion, allowing later readers to draw their own conclusions. We can, for example, reconstruct a link between her son's anxieties about a poisoning witch/mother and her absence from home in spite of her failure to make this connection at the time.

Her interpretations were constantly subjected to the test of the child's behaviour: as she says, they were usually followed by the child illuminating the interpretation with detail in its play or behaviour. Where Klein did not understand something, the child (or adult) would often repeatedly communicate it in different forms until she did. But there is no doubt that insight is not subject to rigid rules and that the meaning of a communication is open to many different interpretations. Klein, just like any other analyst, made her own interpretations in her own way and these would influence the patient and the observations she made next. The analyst's own feelings and insight are an important aspect of the situation which have to be observed by the analyst as objectively as possible. Clearly, it is difficult to convince others that this process has taken place. As the philosophers tell us, observing other people's pain is a very doubtful undertaking, and yet, without some convincing sense of the reality and description of a patient's emotional pain analysts could not work.

The argument continues in some quarters. Analysts claim that their work involves making hypotheses and then testing them; and that these hypotheses can be tested by other analysts working and trained in a similar way. This is what they do with patients on a daily basis.

To give one example, Herbert Rosenfeld, one of Klein's pupils, began analysing homosexual men thinking, as Freud had thought, that paranoia was caused by repressed homosexuality. Following the rules of the analytical method, he analysed the homosexuality of his patients; if the theory were correct, this should have meant that the paranoia would become unnecessary (as a defence against the homosexual feelings and phantasies) and disappear. When he found that analysis of the homosexuality increased the paranoia he concluded that the theory was wrong; that homosexuality was a defence against paranoia rather than the other way round. This approach proved fruitful; analysis of the paranoia reduced the homosexual behaviour and feelings of the patient. This is quite clearly a scientific way of proceeding. It is also repeatable by other analysts.

But psychoanalysis is not scientific in the same way that chemistry is, for example. Psychologists often respond to a similar accusation by seeking to define experiments which they can then test. The interest and value of such insights is then limited to that which is testable by a research project which would be considered respectable by the medical profession or by psychologists. Psychoanalysis does not lend itself to such experiments, though people have tried to create them.

It is not clear what the benefits or disadvantages of being or not being a science are. Understanding of human nature may be demonstrated and conveyed better by Shakespeare than by Truby King, whose 'scientific' methods of bringing up children may have seriously damaged thousands of parents' and children's lives. If 'scientific' means 'leaving out emotions' then therapists cannot be expected to learn much from science. However, even behaviourists have now admitted that they cannot study human behaviour without taking into consideration 'verbalisations' and thoughts, so perhaps the status of emotions and unconscious processes as a proper subject for scientific study may eventually become recognised.

In this case a training which ensures that observers have a good understanding of their own emotions would reasonably be required. During the training process certain ways of thinking and conceptualising are learnt, and these will have an effect on the observations made. Fortunately this process is not totally deterministic: there are people like Klein who can go beyond their teachers and both make new observations and create new theories.

'It's Not Psychoanalysis'

Dr Friedlander, one of the Viennese analysts who arrived with Freud and Anna, talks about 'the difference in Mrs Klein's view as compared with the psycho-analytical theory' (King and Steiner, 1990: 343). In America today many analysts know nothing of Klein and show no interest in her ideas.

Kleinian analysts themselves tend generally to emphasise the continuity of their ideas with those of Freud. Their technique is also quite clearly that which Freud described: the description of Kleinians as 'hard line' conflicts with the idea that they are not using analytical techniques. Klein and her colleagues were not thrown out of the British Psychoanalytical Society and many of Klein's successors (Rosenfeld, Bion, Segal, Joseph, for example) are recognised as amongst the most productive and creative analysts of their generation, particularly in South America and Spain. In addition, Otto Kernberg, a North American ego-psychologist, is just one of many non-Kleinian analysts who do acknowledge the contribution of Klein and the Kleinians to the understanding of psychotic processes.

The Pervasiveness of Phantasy

Many analysts, from the time of the Controversial Discussions to now, have difficulty with Klein's concept of phantasy. During the Controversial Discussions, Dr Sylvia Payne said:

> We all know that memory traces remain of all psychic experiences of any significance but we do not regard unconscious phantasy unless fixated as necessarily cathected [i.e. invested with emotional significance] and dynamic as such throughout life. It seems to me to be against the accepted dynamics of mental functioning to assume that a

certain group of unconscious phantasies is permanently cathected *as such* unless the patient is suffering from a manifest incipient psychosis. It would be an absurdity to imply the latter to the world as a whole. (King and Steiner, 1990: 335)

Kleinians did apply their ideas to the world as a whole. Their view of phantasy was that it was simply more ubiquitous and less abnormal than had been previously thought. They had also come to the belief that everyone has some area of psychotic functioning, though not necessarily a manifest psychosis.

Elizabeth Spillius (1988, II: 6) says that 'the concept of unconscious phantasy . . . is conceived as underlying all thought, rational as well as irrational'; Klein did not think that there was 'a special category of thought and feeling which is rational and appropriate and therefore does not need analysing and a second kind of thought and feeling which is irrational and unreasonable and therefore expresses transference and needs analysing'. This was a new and radical approach to the idea of unconscious phantasy which opened up new avenues for exploration. The idea that powerful phantasies lay behind children's feelings towards their parents, for example, enabled these feelings to be more fully explored rather than simply taken at face value. However reasonable a feeling or thought may appear, the underlying phantasies may repay exploration.

The Role of External Reality as Against Internal Phantasy
Klein has been accused of paying too much attention to internal life at the expense of external reality. In Stern's view, 'Klein postulates the infant's basic subjective experiences as consisting of paranoid, schizoid and depressive positions. These assumed infantile experiences operate outside of ongoing reality perceptions . . . the units of a genetic theory are fantasy-based' (Stern, 1985: 254). This account of Klein's ideas is schematic to the extent of serious misrepresentation. Positions are not 'experiences' but ways of dealing with anxiety and with perceptions of reality. Stern's book in general provides rich and illuminating observations of the relation of an infant with reality and of the complex interactions between neonates and those around them. It confirms the importance to the infant of relationships and shows the infant's ability to relate very sensitively to others from birth: an ability Klein postulated on the basis of her analytical experience.

Klein is categorical about the role of the infant's perception of its own internal processes in creating anxiety and conflict. One role of the mother and later society is that of helping or hindering the child in its management of this internally fuelled anxiety. External reality is very important since it provides evidence or refutations for the child's different conflicting phantasies as well as contributing new challenges and new possibilities for solutions of conflicts. The meaning which the child attaches to external events affects the child's life in very significant ways.

However, Klein had a complex view of the relationship between the child's internal world and the external one. Her attitude is expressed clearly in her paper on 'The Oedipus Complex in the Light of Early Anxieties' (1945) (Klein, 1975, vol. I). She describes the family of Richard, the boy whose analysis she was later to write up into a book. He was brought to analysis because he was unable to attend school, being too frightened of the other children. She describes his symptoms in detail and then mentions his earliest feeding history, his health in infancy and operations he had suffered. She takes considerable care to describe both the relationship between his parents and his relationship with his mother and with his older brother, all of which seem to have been lacking in some way. She goes on to say that 'Though there were difficulties in the family situation – as well as serious difficulties in Richard's early history – in my view the severity of his illness could not be explained by those circumstances alone. As in every case, we have to take into consideration the internal processes resulting from, and interacting with, constitutional as well as environmental factors . . .' (Klein, 1975, I: 372). Certainly, the description of Richard's background, troubled as it is, does not seem so very unusual: if environment in any simple sense were responsible for everything it would be difficult to see why more children are not seriously school-phobic.

Similarly, when she discusses the development of psychoses in her paper about Dick, Klein says that 'Possibly his development was affected by the fact that, though he had every care, no real love was lavished on him, his mother's attitude to him being from the very beginning over-anxious.' Later, however, she writes of Dick's 'apparently constitutional incapacity' to tolerate anxiety and she leaves open the possibility that his mother's 'over-anxious' attitude may have been at least partly a response to something abnormal in Dick, rather than simply a cause of his difficulties.

In these two descriptions Klein makes it clear that she believes that inborn factors are important influences on the child's development. However, she was also quite explicit about the kinds of parental behaviour which would help or hinder the development of a child.

Klein's first paper dealt with the influence on a small boy of bringing him up in a certain way. She described several important guidelines for bringing up children, such as the need to keep them from observation of parental intercourse, the need to allow the child 'to remain for a longer period uninhibited and natural, less interfered with . . . to become conscious of his different instinctive impulses and his pleasure therein without immediately whipping up his cultural tendencies against this ingenuousness . . .' ('Development of a Child': Klein, 1975, I: 26). Later, in a 1936 public lecture on 'Weaning' ((Klein, 1975, vol. I), Klein took considerable space to describe the practices which she thought were harmful to a child. She describes the child's interest not only in sucking but also in his faeces and excreting as early manifestations of sexual feelings there 'from birth onwards'. She says that 'a mother must have a really friendly attitude towards these manifestations of his sexuality' and considers this essential for the development of the child's 'personality and character as well as a satisfactory adult sexuality' (Klein, 1975, I: 301).

She also, in this paper, describes the value to the child and mother of the mother playing with the child rather than leaving it to a nurse and says that:

> A really happy relationship between mother and child can be established only when nursing and feeding the baby is not a matter of duty but a real pleasure to the mother. If she can enjoy it thoroughly, her pleasure will be unconsciously realized by the child, and this reciprocal happiness will lead to a full emotional understanding between mother and child.

She goes on to say how important it is that a mother should recognise that her child is not a possession, 'and that, though he is so small and utterly dependent on her help, he is a separate entity and ought to be treated as an individual human being; she must not tie him too much to herself, but assist him to grow up to independence. . . .' (Klein, 1975, I: 300).

Clearly, Klein is not underestimating the importance, not only of what the mother does for the child, but also of the way she does it. This is the raw material on which the child develops his or her understanding of the world. The actual behaviour and feelings of the mother are capable of creating or inhibiting development in the child. It is characteristic of her that she also allows for the possibility that the mother will not be able to enjoy bringing up her children.

Some people place enormous importance on the role of the parents, to the extent that parents can feel quite threatened and attacked: as if all that happens to their children is entirely their fault. At the same time it is also not uncommon for people to imply that someone's illnesses or difficulties are all their own fault. In each of these situations there may be an attempt to cover up the real lack of knowledge we have about psychological and physical processes by replacing uncertainty with a spurious conviction. We seem to feel it is better to 'know' it was 'us' or 'them' than to admit we do not know how it arose at all.

Klein's belief that constitution may play an important part, though not the only part, in creating conditions in which psychosis or other difficulties can flourish is an important counterweight to the 'blame the parents' view. It is extremely hard living with a psychotic child and parents tend to feel responsible and anxious about this anyway. Given the fact that we do not really know how these conditions arise, it really does seem unnecessarily persecuting to collude with the idea that it is entirely the parents' fault. Genetic factors predisposing to various conditions, from homosexuality to schizophrenia, are constantly being researched and it is possible that some people are born with more difficulty in coping with the demands of reality than others are: Klein's 'constitutional difficulty tolerating anxiety' perhaps. Babies who have difficulties of their own, even if only a greater propensity to painful wind, may behave in such a way as to make it harder for adults to care for them, both emotionally and practically. Equally, where the parents are putting considerable difficulties in the child's way, one child's constitution may make it less able to overcome the parents' mishandling in a way another child could.

Klein is clear that the mother's state of mind is of importance to the child, but she is sympathetic to parents as well as to her patients, conveying a strong awareness of the difficulty we all have, both as children and as parents, in coping with our sadistic, cruel impulses and the anxiety they create. She does not blame parents, even though she was at times very distressed by their behaviour. In a letter to her brother written when she was 19, she says she does not feel equipped to judge his behaviour since she may lack sufficient understanding of it: this humility remained with her in her attitude to parents' relations with their children.

While recognising that Klein felt that certain difficulties might have a constitutional root, it is also important to recognise that she still thought that even the most disturbed people had areas of sanity which could be reached by analysis and could be brought into a therapeutic alliance. Some people who had been subjected to considerable difficulties as children could take from analysis and use the help of the analyst to develop and flourish. Others, apparently from backgrounds with less disturbance, found this harder. We still do not fully understand what it is that children need to enable them to grow up with the fewest possible emotional difficulties. Even less do we know whether parents can provide it or not.

'It's Too Deterministic'

Klein's emphasis on the importance of early life is sometimes interpreted as saying that she believed that nothing that happens later is important at all. This is obviously untrue since every analyst's work with adults is aimed at changing phantasies and structures formed in the earliest period of life. Life too is seen by Kleinians as changing phantasies; the mid-life crisis, for example, is seen as a time when men face the fact that they will not live forever. This challenge can force them to bring to consciousness and reassess some of their primitive phantasies. The result is breakdown if they cannot bear it and/or a new maturity if or when they can.

Sexual relationships and having babies are particular experiences which Klein described as challenging unconscious phantasies and changing them in later life. So too are work relations and work itself, which Klein felt provided an important source of reassurance and support as well as challenge for the individual.

In *Envy and Gratitude*, written towards the end of her life, Klein did express the thought that inborn disposition perhaps puts limits on the *extent* of change possible through analysis (or life). However, to the end she quite explicitly thought that a considerable amount of change was possible for everyone. The limitations only show themselves after many changes have already taken place.

Some people use Klein's insights to explain everything away. This may well give the impression that these ideas are deterministic. However, it is a distortion and a misuse of Klein's work. She was first and foremost an empirical clinician whose interest was in discovering where the child or adult could lead her. Kernberg (1969) accused Kleinian analysts of being over-confident and dominating, but in the *Narrative of a Child Analysis* (see Chapter 3) Klein constantly uses the word 'might' in her interpretations to Richard. Kleinian analysts today emphasise the importance (and difficulty) of maintaining an open mind in each session; they warn of the dangers of attempting to prove theories or to reduce the receptivity of the analyst or therapist in any other way. 'Tolerating uncertainty' is believed by Kleinians to be one of the most important tasks of an analyst, and, by extension, any other Kleinian therapist or counsellor. The temptation to say 'I know' is a snare and a delusion.

The Mind of the Baby in the First 6 Months

The Anna Freud group thought that there was for a baby a period 'in the first months of life' which was 'purely based on the gratification of bodily needs. In the first period when the baby has the urge for the satisfaction of its bodily wishes, routine undertaken by anyone could fulfil this need' (Burlingham, in King and Steiner, 1990: 336). They speak of babies in their first year, and in particular in the first 6 months, as if their impulses and feelings had no meaning except that of narcissistic 'pleasure'.

A more recent version of this idea is described in the American analyst Erna Furman's book, *A Child's Parent Dies* (1974). Talking of the loss of a parent within the first few weeks she points out that:

> a baby a few weeks old will become extremely distressed if his needs are not met adequately and consistently, but we agreed that we had no grounds for assuming that his distress in any way relates to his subjective experience of loss. At a later time, when the baby has only achieved the stage of the need-fulfilling object relationship, that is when the mother's image is cathected only at periods of tensions arising from unfulfilled needs, the loss of the mother would constitute a narcissistic depletion. . . . (Furman, 1974: 41)

The author goes on to describe a young woman, Lucy, whose mother died when she was 10 weeks old. 'Throughout Lucy's childhood and adolescence she suffered from obesity, and from recurring abdominal pains at times of stress.'

Klein, on the other hand, thought that babies (and children) do not have instincts or 'drives' without a phantasy of a relationship which will satisfy them. Klein was clear that babies relate to their parents' bodies and presence even within the first weeks: the distress of a baby who has lost its mother would be quite directly related to phantasies in which the loved object had been attacked as a result of the pain arising from her absence. The baby before 3 months is not likely to be able to hold a sense of loss of a good mother/breast, but is likely to feel full of bad pieces of a bitten up and hated breast/mother, attacking from inside and outside. Lucy's stomach pains seem to bear out this hypothesis.

Equally, Klein did not believe that there is evidence for a period when every baby relates to the mother simply as a narcissistic object or no more than a 'need-fulfilling' object, noticed when she has failed: for a Kleinian this would mean some active denial (on the part of the baby or the observing adult) of the elements of a more whole, loving relationship even if perception of the mother or her breast is not yet integrated. Babies in Kleinian theory are seen as very active and sensitive to external as well as internal conditions from the very beginning. Work since the 1970s on infant development seems to confirm the idea that babies do relate in very complex ways to their surroundings (Stern, 1985).

Esther Bick, and then Martha Harris, ran baby observation courses for many years, partly in response to accusations that there was no evidence for the feeling responses of small babies. Analysts and therapists of all kinds have participated in these observations. The attempt was made to describe without interpretation what was happening to the baby: interpretation could then be discussed in the seminar. These seminars provided a wealth of detailed observations which make it hard to see babies as simply a bundle of undifferentiated instincts, unaware of the difference between people. The minute details of behaviour and movement make up patterns which give rise to convincing interpretations. Such close observation of babies with and without their parents does suggest that babies react to their surroundings in a complex feeling way, and that some parents are realistically sensitive to this. However, it is difficult to interpret babies' feelings on the basis of their behaviour or body language, and parents' own self-confidence and range of accessible feelings influence their interpretations, just as an observer's training and sensitivity influence theirs.

It is interesting that some mothers seem to see their babies as actively responding to the environment in general and to themselves in particular; others do not believe their babies notice them or distinguish them or have feelings. Some mothers and fathers believe it would be arrogant or foolish of them to assume that their babies relate any differently to them; some even think that anyone else would be a better parent to the child than they are; while others are sure that their child behaves differently with different care-givers even if they cannot prove it. Some parents leave their babies when they are small with apparently no concern that the child will notice: others do not.

Aggressive Babies

Many people opposed and still oppose Klein's view that a small baby may have powerful feelings of aggression not only towards its mother in general but even towards her breast at an age when the baby is too small to have a perception of her as a whole person. Fairbairn, Winnicott and Bowlby all took issue with her over this.

Teaching about Klein for many years, I have found that the idea that the small baby has feelings of hatred and aggressiveness from the beginning is extremely unpalatable, particularly among those who like to see the baby as the innocent victim of a cruel world. Those who have given birth to babies themselves tend in my experience to have a view more accepting of Klein's. The idea that a baby has only good, loving feelings towards its mother does not really stand up to nights pacing backwards and forwards with a baby who is screaming and will not be comforted, or who sometimes turns away from the breast and screams for no apparent reason. Clearly, there may be a reason, but it is not a simple matter of being a bad parent.

In 'Notes on Some Schizoid Mechanisms' (Klein, 1975, vol. III), Klein spells out her agreements and disagreements with Fairbairn. She says he underrates 'the role which hatred and aggression play from the beginning of life. As a result of this approach, he does not give enough weight to the importance of early anxiety and conflict and their dynamic effects on development' (Klein, 1975, III: 4). Klein's view is that the child's aggression gives rise to anxiety *since it conflicts with the child's powerfully loving impulses*. This counterbalance to the child's aggression is sometimes overlooked.

Winnicott and Bowlby both in their different ways objected to Klein's view of the normality of aggressive feelings in the baby and also in the mother. This has far-reaching consequences in terms of the role of both the parents. For the followers of Winnicott, the baby is a far more benign and victimised creature than for Klein. The splits in the ego and the internal world are recognised, but without emphasis on the active way in which the child (and eventually the adult) maintains and creates these splits. From the Kleinian point of view, not only does this omit an important aspect of the child's or adult's control over these processes, but it also has the practical effect that there seems little prospect of regaining control over the splitting process and mending the splits. In 'Notes on Some Schizoid Mechanisms', Klein takes up Winnicott's view that the baby at first is unintegrated: she says she finds this quite convincing but immediately she speaks of it as a 'disintegration' which alternates with a tendency to integration. The difference is crucial.

Winnicott, in the introduction to his book *The Child, the Family and the Outside World* (1964), writes for 'the ordinary good mother with her husband in support' and about the good she does 'simply through being devoted to her infant'. By comparison with Klein, Winnicott's approach is enormously idealising of mothers and their situation. He speaks of a mother's 'natural tendencies' to do the right thing, and this was an important counter to theories of people like Truby King who told mothers not to pick their children up when they cried. But mothers often scoff at the idea that they have such 'natural tendencies' and Klein's descriptions of the relations between mothers and children are much closer to reality for all the parents I have ever met.

In his book, Winnicott implies a strong disagreement with all that Klein and her successors have described about the processes of projection, in which hated and 'bad' aspects of the self and the objects/people inside are projected into or seen in people outside. He writes as if mothers only ever saw their babies as good and loving, when it is clear that many mothers hate their babies at times, forget them at others, and have very conflicting and troubling feelings a lot of the time. By idealising, Winnicott becomes quite persecuting to real mothers, who find no recognition of their 'badness' or discomfort and only a strong implication that a real woman, an 'ordinary devoted mother', does not mind when her baby wets her or simply feels pleasure and excitement when the milk comes in – which can be an excruciatingly painful experience. The mother's actual feelings of love towards her baby may seem puny, insufficient and short-lived by comparison with Winnicott's descriptions, whereas it is possible to imagine that one could be a better mother than the mothers Klein describes.

Both Bowlby and Winnicott see the father's role as protecting the mother from the outside world but they do not see him as protecting the mother from the child and the child from the mother. Klein believed that the father's support and help is felt by the child to be crucial in restoring the health, goodness, happiness and babies of the mother after the child's phantasied attacks on her. If the aggression and phantasies of attack between mother and child are not fully recognised, as they are not by Bowlby and Winnicott, this role is also not acknowledged. This is consistent with the different approaches Winnicott and Klein have towards separation. Klein emphasises the Oedipal relation with the father as crucial for healthy separation between mother and child; Winnicott emphasises the role of the 'transitional object' (or 'Linus blanket') which is under the child's control and is inanimate.

The Development of Sexuality

The Viennese analysts during the Controversial Discussions also accused Klein of differing enormously with Freud over the issue of the development of the super-ego and of sexuality. Klein did differ from Freud in these areas.

In 'The Oedipus Complex in the Light of Early Anxieties' (1945) (Klein, 1975, vol. I), Klein used Richard's material to describe the development of the Oedipus complex in a boy and her material on Rita to illustrate the Oedipus complex in a girl. At the end of this paper she describes the differences between her view and Freud's on the development of sexuality. Below are summarised just some of these.

She agreed that oral, anal and genital interests followed each other, but she thought that they overlapped and built upon each other more than Freud did. Freud had thought that during the phase from about 3 to 5 years old 'only one genital, namely the male one, comes into account. What is present, therefore, is not the primacy of the genitals but the primacy of the phallus' (Freud, 1975, XIX: 142). Klein, however, thought that 'infants of both sexes experience genital desires directed towards their mother and father, and they have an unconscious knowledge of the vagina as well as of the penis' (Klein, 1975, I: 416).

Freud also thought that guilt only entered into the child's experience after the super-ego had developed, which he thought happened after the breakdown of the Oedipus complex, under threat of castration from the father: in other words, after the age of about 6. Klein's view was that:

> The earliest feelings of guilt in both sexes derive from the oral-sadistic desires to devour the mother, and primarily her breasts . . . It is therefore in infancy that feelings of guilt arise. Guilt does not emerge when the Oedipus Complex comes to an end, but is rather one of the factors which from the beginning mould its course and affect its outcome. (Klein, 1975, I: 417).

She also found that the super-ego arose much earlier, under the sway of oral feelings. This meant that the earliest super-ego was a devouring, biting figure, the basis of the 'gnawing' conscience and 'biting' criticism. Later the child takes in its parents (and other significant people) under the influence of urethral desires; then anal and finally genital.

> Thus, although the super-ego corresponds in many ways to the actual people in the young child's world, it has various components and features which reflect the phantastic image in his mind. All the factors which have a bearing on his object relations play a part from the beginning in the building-up of the super-ego.
>
> The first introjected object, the mother's breast, forms the basis of the super-ego. Just as the relation to the mother's breast precedes and strongly influences the relation to the father's penis, so the relation to the introjected mother affects the whole course of super-ego development. Some of the most important features of the super-ego, whether loving and protective or destructive and devouring, are derived from the early maternal components of the super-ego. (Klein, 1975, I: 417)

Freud thought that a girl had a long 'pre-Oedipal' phase of exclusive attachment to her mother; that during her phallic phase, in which she becomes aware of the clitoris, she wants a penis from her mother. He did not think that the girl discovered the vagina until womanhood. He thought the girl turns from the mother in resentment and hatred because she has not given her a penis. Her discovery that her mother does not have a penis contributes to her turning to her father, from whom she hopes to receive a penis. It is only when she discovers she cannot have this that she settles for the desire to have a baby from him.

We have already made it clear how much Klein challenged this. She did not think that the girl was as concerned as Freud thought she was at the discovery that her mother did not have a penis of her own. She thought that:

> The unconscious theory that her mother contains the admired and desired penis of the father underlies, in my experience, many of the phenomena that Freud described as the relation of the girl to the phallic mother.
> The girl's oral desires for her father's penis mingle with her first genital desires to receive that penis. These genital desires imply the wish to receive children from her father, which is also borne out by the equation 'penis = child'. The feminine desire to internalise the penis and to receive a child from her father invariably precedes the wish to possess a penis of her own. (Klein, 1975, I: 418)

Personally, I have never been convinced by the idea that children have an innate awareness of the vagina and penis. My own interpretation of the case material given by Klein and some other analysts is that there is nothing which is not consistent with a different view, that the child creates a phantasy of the penis and vagina out of their experience of the breast, nipple and mouth and their mother's ability to produce milk and other good things. The penis–nipple equation is clearly shown by the two small boys I know who referred to their penises using their word for a nipple. The fantasy of a 'feeding penis' to me seems to be clearly based on the phantasy of a nipple attributed to a man, just as the fantasy of the 'vagina with teeth' seems to be based on the phantasy of a mouth. However, I am aware that in the consulting room other elements come into play which are not described in the writing up and Klein had sources of evidence available to her in her clinical work which I do not have.

The Death Instinct

Kernberg (1969), discussing the work of the Kleinians, says that there is a 'total lack of clinical evidence' in support of the theory of an inborn death instinct, though he does not address Freud's own evidence for it. However, he considers that the rest of Klein's ideas neither stand nor fall by this concept and considers it could easily be dropped without damaging the rest of the theory.

Hanna Segal is the leading Kleinian analyst today. Her views have developed over the years and differ from Klein on several issues, for example, her understanding of symbolism. Hanna Segal has made explicit and extended the concept of the death instinct, translating it into more pragmatic terms. She believes that the child is from birth subject to conflicts between a desire to annihilate everything (including life itself) and a desire to live. Talking to Jonathan Miller in 1983 she said: 'To me the death instinct is not a biological drive to return to the inorganic (as Freud described it) but it is a psychological wish to annihilate the sudden change brought about by birth' (Miller, 1983: 255). This view is consistent with Klein's observations and Hanna Segal thinks that Klein in fact saw it in this way. Part of the difference is to do with changes in approach: the whole theory of 'instincts' has undergone modification since Freud and Klein were writing.

'Klein is Reactionary'

In the early 1970s it was fashionable to dismiss all psychoanalysis as politically reactionary: as attempting to make people fit society instead of changing society. This view changed in Britain as people began to study psychoanalytical writings more seriously, beginning with the work of Lacan. It became evident that Klein's ideas had radical implications. For example, she rejected the idea that all women envied men the possession of a penis: a notion which was used at the time to bolster male chauvinism. Her observations of envy (in both sexes) towards the mother's creativity challenged the idea that women could be defined by their lack of a penis and provided new ammunition for those who wished to assert the importance of the female body (and mind) for its positive attributes. Some of these issues are taken up in J. Segal (1979).

Klein's view is still considered politically reactionary in some circles because she cannot be said to blame 'society' for the ills of children and adults. She was too aware of the conflicts within each one of us: conflicts which we project into the abstraction 'society' and into different aspects of it. Her view is complex and does not sit comfortably with the splitting and idealisation which motivates some political action.

However, when it comes to work within the health service, for example, Klein's influence is enormously challenging of the status quo. The insistence on the need for professional consultation for health workers to help them with the emotional stresses of their jobs, for example, is a great challenge to the system, and one which gains much momentum from the work of Kleinian therapists and theorists. The work of one of these, Isabel Menzies-Lyth (1988) has radical implications for the treatment of both patients and nurses in hospitals and has led to important work in other institutions and organisations.

Kleinian psychoanalysts are also among the most active founders of Psychoanalysts against Nuclear Weapons. A belief in the biological nature of aggression or of the capacity to experience gratitude or envy does not mean a belief that we are all doomed to destroy ourselves. Kleinian analysts such as Hanna Segal argue that it is the responsibility of psychoanalysts to speak out and to expose the unconscious aggression and destructiveness beneath our foreign and 'defence' policies: anything else is to collude in the potential destruction of ourselves and the whole world.

Do We Need Psychoanalysis at All?

People sometimes talk or write as if analysis has gone out of fashion: the behaviourist school in the UK is and always has been strong and there is a feeling that psychoanalysis is an extravagance, a self-indulgence.

There are several reasons why some of us think that it is important that psychoanalysis continues. One is that five-times-a-week psychoanalysis is the only way of really understanding how the mind works at the level of the deepest anxieties, particularly the psychotic ones. The insights of analysts can then be used in other contexts, in the work of counsellors, teachers, nurses, doctors or by parents. There have been vast changes in our understanding of both children and adults as a result of the work of analysts and analytically inspired people over the past fifty years and more. Childcare, nursing and teaching practices have been enormously influenced by the insights derived from analysis.

Analysis of both adults and children has also brought to our attention the need for a different way of handling the losses children suffer, for example, when their parents are in hospital or leave home or die. It is such insights into the mourning process which help counsellors to work with adults who are disturbed by past losses. The work of analysts offers insight into the process of once-a-week therapy and counselling and can help therapists and counsellors to pay more attention to the aspects of counselling which can bring about most change.

There are also some conditions which can only be changed by analysis. For example, psychotic conditions including schizophrenia, tics in children which may be a sign of severe hidden disturbance, and autism, are all very resistant to 'tender loving care' or any other more active treatment and may only respond to analysis five times a week. In addition, some physical conditions such as asthma and eczema may be considerably helped by analysis.

The fact that analysis is expensive and out of the reach of most people is no reason for depriving those who can pay for it or who can obtain it free. Acting upon envy is seldom a good idea. More support for analysts and better organisation of the health service so that analysis is available to more people would be more beneficial. Analysis could be offered to people in vulnerable positions, such as those working in prisons, in the police force or hospitals, particularly mental hospitals, for example. However, this seems a Utopian demand. Meanwhile, we have to make do with what we have which, at least in London, may include psychoanalytical supervision of our work. There are also low-cost analyses available with analysts in training; in addition, many analysts take some patients at very low fees or work in organisations which can provide analysis free under certain circumstances, subsidising this work by their private practice.

'Klein's Ideas are Incomprehensible'

This chapter concludes with an illustration of how condensed theoretical formulations may fail to reveal the very human and alive interactions between Kleinian analyst and patient. Many people find Klein's ideas difficult or incomprehensible and cannot imagine how children can understand them. This passage, from *The Work of Hanna Segal*, describes a session with a little girl just under 4 years old: the session itself is a delightful example of the work of a child analyst.

> I was then having supervision on this child with Melanie Klein and, being in a hurry to present some rather difficult sessions at the end of the week, I wanted to summarize for her very briefly the sessions at the beginning of the week. I said that on Monday it seemed the little girl was preoccupied with a phantasy of my pregnancy over the weekend, and then, taking a deep breath, I said 'And I interpreted to her that an introjection done under a preponderance of envious greed leads to the fragmentation of the internal object, fragmentation of self, internal persecution, confusion, a loss of identity, particularly sexual identity.' I saw then that Melanie Klein looked at me with a really shocked expression, and she said, very quietly, 'I think I would rather like to see this session: I do not quite see how you interpreted all that to a child under four.' I then told her the session in detail and she agreed with the line of interpretation.
>
> The little girl had come into the room. She looked at my abdomen and said, 'You've got fatter over the weekend.' She then showed me a little purse, of which she was obviously very proud. She then went to

a drawer and pulled out a brown paper bag, which the previous week she had filled up with her toys. She looked at the bag and said, with real fury, 'Your purses are always bigger than my purses.' I interpreted then that she thought my tummy was always bigger than her tummy and she thought mine was full of babies, like the paper bag, and that was why it was so fat. She then filled the basin with water, tore the paper bag into shreds, and put the torn bag and all the animals into the basin. She also put her own purse there, saying, 'Anyway, they're not your toys – they're *my* toys.' She started swirling the water around angrily and put in bits of soap, making the water cloudy. As in the past, putting things into this water basin often represented introjection, and since she accompanied it by saying 'They're my toys,' I interpreted to her that she wanted to take my tummy and my babies inside her tummy to make it into her babies – but she was so angry that it was mine to begin with, that in taking it in she tore it all into pieces. Then she looked at me less angrily and said that on Sunday she had had a nasty tummyache. I related the nasty tummyache to her having phantasied that she had torn off bits of my tummy and babies inside her, and the bits were angry and making her hurt. Then she looked at the basin and said 'Oh, what a muddle' (feeling muddled is something occasionally insightfully complained of). I interpreted to her that she put the bits of soap in to make the water cloudy because she did not want to know which bits inside her were hers and which she thought she had stolen from me; that she then felt this muddle both as a tummyache in her tummy and as a muddle in her thoughts. She did not know which thoughts were hers and which came from me. She then started looking for her purse in the water and became very anxious and angry when she could not readily find it 'in the muddle'. I then interpreted that when she so much wanted to have my insides inside her and all muddled up with her, and was also so angrily tearing them to bits, then she became very frightened that she could not properly feel her own body. She went on feeling in the basin with one hand and with the other searching between her legs for her genital. I said that this feeling of not being able to find her own things made her feel sometimes that she could not find her own 'baby-hole' because in her mind she felt it was so muddled up with mine. After this interpretation she readily found the purse, took it out of the water, and showed great relief.

At no time in the session did I have the feeling that my interpretations were too complicated for her or that she could not follow them. And though she verbalized little in this session, in the next she spoke quite freely of her anxieties that either I or her mother would go on producing new babies, and of her envy and wish to be a 'mummy full of babies' herself. (H. Segal, 1981: 34–5)

As Segal says, in summarizing such interpretations 'one may sound as though one were talking a language which would be complete gibberish to the child.' Klein did not speak gibberish, but in summary her ideas can sound very peculiar indeed.

5

The Overall Influence of Melanie Klein

Influence of Klein's Theories

Melanie Klein's influence has been considerable but often unrecognised. In 1973 during a dinner party in Manchester I asked a student doctor what, if anything, he had been taught about psychoanalysis. He told me that it was 'out of date' and 'had been disproved'. Later in the evening he related enthusiastically something he had recently learnt in lectures: 'Did we know that babies were supposed to get depressed at around 3 months, and that if they didn't there was something wrong?' He was somewhat put out when we told him gently that he was quoting the ideas of Melanie Klein: ideas she had discovered during the course of her work as a psychoanalyst.

The work of Klein and her colleagues and students has been influential in the fields of psychoanalysis, psychotherapy and counselling and in a wider context of therapeutic communities and social work. Many of the ideas we now take for granted about children, the importance of childhood and the effects of experiences and relationships in childhood have in fact arisen through the work of analysts including Klein.

Klein's Influence on Psychoanalysis

The influence of Kleinian ideas on the work of British, European and South American analysts is far greater than Klein's influence on the ideas of analysts in the United States. It is not clear why this is. American analysts do not allow non-medical members, but they have embraced Anna Freud (Grosskurth says that many American analysts are convinced that Anna Freud had a medical degree, which she did not). Many Viennese analysts went to the USA when Freud came to England; these analysts were on the whole opposed to Klein and discouraged attention to her ideas.

The direction taken by most American analysts and therapists has been away from the importance of unconscious processes and towards conscious ones. The ideas of the school of ego-psychology perhaps fit better with American ideas about the primacy of the self than Klein's ideas of the primacy of phantasies involving guilt, dependence, care for others and the destructiveness of envy and greed.

In many countries there is a move among analysts away from five-times-a-week analysis. The Kleinians oppose this, in particular for the analysis of trainees, but they are frequently under pressure to permit it. Kleinians feel strongly that analysis should ensure as far as possible that there are no hidden areas of deep or psychotic disturbance before a student analyst is permitted to qualify: without five-times-a-week analysis they do not feel this can be achieved. In order to fund this, Kleinian analysts often charge a lower fee per session than their counterparts in the USA and Europe.

Child Analysis and Child Psychotherapy
The analysis of children, particularly in Britain, continues to develop under the influence of the ideas of Klein and present-day Kleinians. Child analysts of the school of Anna Freud still keep to a considerable extent separate from Kleinians but there is some cross-fertilisation of ideas.

As psychotherapy of children has become more available, it seems that children with greater difficulties are brought to therapy, and understanding of the extreme effects of various kinds of deprivation or ill-treatment on such children is growing. As we understand more of children's needs for containment, understanding of the role of adults in children's lives increases.

Klein's Influence on Counsellors
Some of the theories of counsellors and psychotherapists in the USA have been developed either under the influence of, or in opposition to, American psychoanalysts. The Rogerian 'person-centred' school, for example, seems to have been set up to counteract dogmatic and self-opinionated attitudes attributed (with however much or little justification) to American psychoanalysts. As a Kleinian-influenced counsellor, I find I have more in common with some 'person-centred' counsellors than with the attitudes described, for example, by Hilda Bruch (1974) in *Eating Disorders* as those of American psychoanalysts.

Many counsellors in Britain have been influenced more by American counselling theorists than by British analysts. Counsellors belonging to the British Association for Counselling who claim a 'psychodynamic' orientation are in a minority; of these, by no means all would claim allegiance to (or perhaps even knowledge of) Kleinian ideas. There is a certain amount of suspicion of analysis and analytical therapists, sometimes based on bad experiences with individuals, sometimes on prejudice or on the mistaken belief that all analysts are like those illustrated in American films.

Psychoanalytically influenced therapists and counsellors have a considerable respect for intellectual thought, considering that it can contain and express emotional states without destroying them. Bion's idea of containment (Bion, 1967), based on Klein's work, includes both a warm accepting presence and the use of words to convey and hold significant emotional meaning and truth. Thought is also considered to be the basis of reality-testing and vitally important for rational action. Although there is a recognition of the dangers of misusing thinking as a defence against experiencing, Kleinians are concerned to avoid denigrating the processes of thinking itself. This can lead to mutual distrust between psychodynamic counsellors and some counsellors who are more suspicious of intellectual thought, appear to mistrust it and feel that it threatens the counselling process as they understand it.

Klein and Psychotherapy

Although Klein said she could not and would not do it herself, many of the insights of Kleinian analysts can be used in psychotherapy. In the UK, the Tavistock Clinic has been influential in training psychotherapists and disseminating ideas about psychotherapy and counselling, many of which originated with Klein. The Institute of Marital Studies within the Tavistock Clinic influenced the training of Relate counsellors who make up a considerable number of British counsellors. However, the Tavistock Clinic is also influenced by other analysts such as Balint, Winnicott and Bowlby, who all had strong disagreements with Klein or she with them. Similarly, the Westminster Pastoral Foundation (WPF), which trains many psychotherapists and counsellors, includes on its staff many therapists who disagree with some of Klein's ideas and do not work in a Kleinian way, though in many ways their training does conform with Kleinian standards. For example, the WPF insists on therapists in training being in analysis or therapy themselves, which Relate still does not. Some of the other training organisations for psychotherapists and counsellors include Kleinians on their staff: some do not. The Society for Analytical Psychology (followers of Jung) teach Kleinian ideas to their therapists.

We have already described Klein's ideas about the way sessions are conducted. Kleinian therapists of any kind are very aware that everything they say and do, and every detail of the room and even the building, has unconscious symbolic meaning to their patient or client. This has practical consequences in terms of the setting for therapy and counselling which are applied today as they were when Klein formulated them.

In addition, Kleinian approaches to the work itself may be distinctive. Kleinians are less afraid of disturbing people's defences than they are of leaving people alone with hidden fears and anxieties which could be reduced if *the therapist* could face the anxiety involved. They feel that the patient has to live with the damage caused by anxieties and the defences against them, whether they are conscious or not. They see the therapist's job as to modify anxieties and emotions by acknowledging and sharing them and demonstrating that they are bearable; not to collude with covering them up and leaving the client alone with them. Other schools of therapy support the opposite view: they encourage therapists not to disturb defences and see them as less damaging and destructive than Kleinians do.

Two examples illustrate the difference of the Kleinian approach.

A non-Kleinian therapist was talking with a Kleinian about a young man with a life-threatening condition who said he wanted to buy a very fast car and drive it 'to destruction'. The therapist had not asked the boy if he had thoughts of suicide. The Kleinian felt that the boy was making it very clear that he had such thoughts and that it would have been a good idea to ask him. She also thought the boy might have been testing the therapist to see if she could cope with his suicidal feelings, and that the therapist had quite clearly conveyed to him, by not picking up his clear hints, that she could not. The other said she worked in a different way; she was respecting his defences. Since he had not explicitly said he was suicidal she did not raise it.

Another non-Kleinian therapist described how he had talked with a family about their feelings concerning the imminent death of the father. The parents said they felt they had accepted it and it did not worry them any more. One of the children said 'What about us?' Neither the parents nor the therapist said anything; when challenged the therapist justified his silence by saying 'They had had enough; they couldn't take any more.' A listening Kleinian felt that it was the therapist who could not 'take it'; the children had to and they were being left alone with it. She felt that the therapist was actually being cruel to the children and abandoning them without realising it.

In this sense Kleinians in comparison with some other therapists have a more robust and trusting belief in the client's ability to face his or her internal reality, however painful. They also have a more uncompromising conviction that reality is worth facing. This arises from the belief that perception is based on unconscious phantasy, and that reality-testing of such phantasies takes away the very primitive, frightening or even monstrous phantasies which attach themselves to the unknown and the unspeakable. The result is that fears are reduced by naming them and bringing them into the open.

The belief that defences never actually work also contributes to the Kleinian willingness to challenge them. Unconscious fears do not go away however hard we will them to: they simply reappear in other, often more damaging forms. Those who have a less strong conviction in the power and reality of unconscious processes have less motivation for distrusting the effectiveness of conscious defences.

Work with Groups

Klein did not approve of either family therapy or group therapy and some Kleinian therapists view both of these with some suspicion. Some of those who work with groups use Kleinian ideas, particularly as worked out by Bion, while others do not. The Institute of Group Analysis teaches the ideas of Klein and Bion.

Practical Effects of a Kleinian Approach to Therapy and Counselling

The Setting

Freud had already established the basic guidelines for the analytical setting, though he did not always keep to them. The work of Klein gave an explanation as to why it was so important, and previous chapters have already discussed this. Present-day Kleinian therapists of all kinds tend to follow Klein in emphasising the importance of the setting.

Kleinians believe that internal security depends upon good experiences of dependence on a reliable person. It is only with such a person that the deepest anxieties can be held and explored. It is only if the person constantly demonstrates his or her capacity to survive undamaged that the phantasies of destroying and attacking the loved breast/mother can be activated, brought into contact with reality and modified.

It does not feel safe to be dependent upon someone who is unreliable and changing. Kleinian therapists of all kinds attempt to keep conditions as constant as possible and take up with the patient or client any changes in time, place or setting which do unavoidably occur. Patients and clients are often not only strongly affected by such changes, but they are astonished at the extent of their reaction. It may take months before they will admit that they mind missing sessions, or they mind if a therapist is late or absent for any reason – and that they have always minded.

Kleinians are also very aware of holidays as times when patients are likely to react badly in one way or another. Picking up a client's feelings about a holiday may help to locate problems around parting and loss and the ways the client reacts to these, which can be of enormous importance for the client's sense of inner security, not only over the holiday but also in the long term.

For similar reasons, a long preparation time is allowed for finishing a series of therapy sessions: work on the ending is begun from the beginning, if the number of sessions is limited. This work on the ending is considered vital since it is processes of loss which stimulate much of development. How loss is handled affects long-term mental stability and security and a Kleinian therapist would consider it an important part of their responsibility to help their clients with this processs.

The Relation with the Analyst/Therapist

No Socialising We looked at this in Chapter 4 when discussing the criticism that Kleinians do not behave like 'human beings'. Here we take up the implications for present-day practice.

Kleinian therapists generally avoid social chat in sessions. It is possible to do this while conveying a warm interest in the client and in the work being done together. Sometimes this leads to resentment or complaint from clients, but this itself can be taken up and considered as part of the relationship.

A young man constantly complained that the counsellor did not begin with chat but waited to see what he would bring to the session that day. The counsellor told him why she did it and why she felt it was more important for both of them to bear his discomfort than to relieve it immediately. She explored his complaints in many different ways. One aspect of them was his desire to make her behave as he thought she should behave and his anger when she had her own ideas about how she should be in order to help him. This was a complaint he had against many other people. Another aspect was his resentment that the relationship was professional: he had strong feelings about this. He also had a belief that discomfort and frustration were 'bad for his health'. This had many implications in all his relationships.

For another client, difficulty at the beginning of the session seemed to be related to a feeling that he had nothing to say and 'could not communicate'. In fact, he was communicating a lot by his gestures and behaviour, and this needed to be acknowledged: he was devaluing a whole area of his experience by claiming that only words counted. His conviction that something was wrong with his ability to communicate was true and needed to be explored but it was to do with a discontinuity between words and feelings. The counsellor's refusal to 'socialise' brought this into the open and enabled client and counsellor to look at it.

Since any statement or opinion expressed by the analyst or therapist will be interpreted by the patient in an unpredictable way, Kleinian therapists tend to avoid social chat for this reason too. By restricting themselves as far as possible to considering the client's words and behaviour and by offering understanding, not reassurance or any of the other forms of gratification of relationships, the Kleinian therapist aims to provide a solid, reliable kind of holding which does not increase the client's confusion.

Physical Contact   Physical contact is also kept to a minimum during Kleinian therapy. Kleinians are aware of the sexual and other interpretations which clients (often unconsciously) put on physical contact and which cannot be predicted. Touching and hugging may be experienced as invasive and threatening as well as sexually arousing. Projection of the client's own sexual arousal into the therapist can give rise to disturbing beliefs that the therapist is attempting to seduce the client. Any of these responses can frighten the patient either consciously or unconsciously. Stroking or hugging can also reinforce a phantasy that the therapist is using the client for his or her own gratification. Even if a therapist means to hug in good faith, there is no way of knowing how the client will interpret it.

Sometimes, of course, therapists do have difficulty with their own feelings towards clients. These may arise from the therapist and/or from the client. Unconscious sexual attraction towards the client may affect the therapist's judgement. In addition, some people can put a therapist or counsellor under enormous pressure to react to them in a sexual fashion: this is well recognised nowadays with, for example, some people who have been abused as children. (It is an example of the effectiveness of a potentially very destructive projective identification.) The temptation to repeat the abuse of such a client is disturbingly strong. An absolute taboo on physical expression of feelings may help the therapist to contain his or her own impulses in such a situation until better judgement is regained. If a therapist in this situation did, for example, even hug or stroke the client, the client would not be totally wrong in believing that it was for the therapist's gratification rather than in the cause of therapy. The ban on physical contact is a protection not only for the client but also for the therapist.

With patients who suffer from psychotic episodes, in particular, there are difficulties with the interpretation the patient would give to attempts at touching. Since affection and hatred may be quite confused in such people at times, any attempt to come close may unpredictably be felt as extremely seductive or extremely threatening: it can produce a physically dangerous counter-attack. At other times an approach would be experienced in a more 'normal' way. However, Kleinian analysts may shake hands with patients before long holiday breaks.

Self-disclosure Some of the issues involved in self-disclosure were discussed in Chapter 4. There are other reasons for avoiding it. When a therapist avoids telling his or her client about him/herself both have more chance of finding out what the therapist stands for in the client's mind. For example, if a client asks if the therapist has children the therapist would normally find some way of exploring what this means to the client without giving an answer. Leaving this question open enables client and therapist to seek some understanding of the way the client imagines the therapist, and the implications of this for the way they see the world. In addition, it becomes easier to convince the client that his or her perception is not simply based on reality and actual knowledge, but on something he or she has brought to the situation.

In the opinion of Kleinians, self-disclosure by the therapist can cause other problems for the client. There can be the feeling that the therapist is using the client to contain their problems. A client said 'I stopped going to that counsellor: she was always talking about her problems with her daughter.'

There can be rivalry between client and therapist for time and space. A therapist may feel a particular urge to reveal him/herself to a client who has been brought up with relationships where the client took care of an adult who should have been the care giver. Self-revelation shifts the focus from the client to the therapist and deprives the client of attention. Some clients slip easily into a situation where they appear to be doing the looking after: 'I went to see him because I felt he needed me: I felt sorry for him because he was ill.' This client had responded to her therapist's revelation of his own illness with an attempt to care for him instead of herself. When she was a child this client had taken care of her alcoholic father in the same way: then, as now, she attempted unsuccessfully to deny that she had any needs of her own.

Self-revelation is tempting when a therapist cannot bear the difference between the client and the therapist. The therapist wants to say 'Me too!' or 'Don't be angry with me for being OK, I'm just as bad as you are really, look, I'll show you.' Such a situation needs to be explored rather than defused by the therapist revealing their own problems. Self-disclosure would prevent the feeling of tension being explored more fully: a chance to recognise a feeling of being left out, ignored, despised or envied, for example, may be missed. This feeling may belong to the client and could be given back and acknowledged rather than expropriated by the therapist.

A woman said 'As I left I turned round and saw my therapist looking at me with a terrible expression on his face. I asked what was the matter and he said "You really disgust me".' Another client said 'My therapist told me that I gave him an erection. He said it didn't matter as long as he didn't do anything about it.' Both of these clients were very distressed by what the therapist had said, or what they thought he had said. A Kleinian would quite definitely consider that self-revelation of this kind was unprofessional. Many other therapists would agree: perhaps even the therapists who were quoted or misquoted.

A ban on all self-revelation by a therapist makes it easier to ensure that clients or patients do not go away with the impression of such things having been said to them. It would also make it easier to convince the client that this cannot have been said if the client has imagined it. Kleinian therapists are very much opposed to self-revelation partly because of the real imposition onto the patient or client; partly because of the ease with which serious misunderstandings occur.

Self-disclosure by a therapist may also not produce the effect the therapist hopes. A client said how her counsellor could not possibly understand how awful it was to be in therapy. Instead of exploring this, the (new) counsellor told her that on the contrary she had been in therapy for several years before becoming a counsellor. The client then announced that this obviously meant that the counsellor was too mad to help her.

Working with the Transference For Kleinian analysts the symbolic meaning of the analyst to the patient is the focus of the work. It is transference interpretations which are considered the most effective. Counsellors influenced by Klein are amongst those who emphasise the importance of the 'here and now', though Kleinians may use the way this relationship appears to be rooted in the past when talking about the 'here and now' relationship. This link with the past can bring relief to the client though it can also be misused by therapist or client to distract attention from the present.

Freud described transference very clearly in *Remembering, Repeating and Working Through*:

> the patient does not say that he remembers that he used to be defiant and critical towards his parents' authority; instead he behaves in that way to the doctor. He does not remember how he came to a helpless and hopeless deadlock in his infantile sexual researches; but he produces a mass of confused dreams and associations, complains that he cannot succeed in anything and asserts that he is fated never to carry through what he undertakes. He does not remember having been intensely ashamed of certain sexual activities and afraid of their being found out; but he makes it clear that he is ashamed of the treatment on which he is now embarked and tries to keep it secret from everybody. And so on. (Freud, 1975, XII: 150)

Klein's work made it clear that both children and adults 'transfer' onto the person of the analyst feelings and phantasies they have about their parents. They use phantasies derived from their relationship with those who cared for them early in their lives to understand and make sense of the analyst just as they do with anyone else. The analyst plays a part in their lives and the task is to find out what this part is, and how it works, in order to modify it. The modified phantasies are then used to understand people in the outside world and the client's relationships in general improve. The improvement of their relationship with themselves and the phantasy 'people inside them' also liberates their creativity and their intellect.

It is clear from work with children that the feelings directed at the analyst are not exactly the same as those directed at the parents. Trude was not as frightened of attacking Klein as she was of attacking her mother. She could show her aggressive fantasies towards her mother's body clearly in her behaviour towards Klein, whereas with her mother she was very careful and clinging. Fears of damaging, hurting or destroying the analyst or other therapist will not be as strong. This means that destructive or attacking phantasies can find expression more easily than they can outside the therapeutic relationship. In therapy they can be understood, brought into contact with reality and worked through while the therapist makes the situation feel safe enough.

Klein felt it was very important to analyse both the negative transference and the positive one, if the conflicts between love and hatred are to be resolved. In practical terms, this means that Kleinians pay close attention to any signs of feelings or phantasies, positive or negative, towards the therapist.

When, for example, clients start complaining about their doctor or their neighbour or some other person in their life a Kleinian therapist is likely to wonder if any of the complaints could be covertly directed at the therapist. The need to make this link is important, not just because it is true and real and may uncover a real complaint against the therapist, but because by splitting the perception of the therapist in this way the client is splitting themselves. The 'nice client' who does not complain about the therapist is different from the 'nasty client' or 'victim client' who complains about someone else. This level of splitting is insecure and depletes the client, removing some of their power to take control of events in a straightforward manner.

By picking up hints of feelings towards the therapist and by attempting to understand them, many powerful messages are conveyed to the client. Not only can the client or patient be given some help in understanding their own impulses towards the therapist, but the therapist conveys the idea that it is possible to think about both negative and positive feelings with the person concerned rather than pretend that they are not there. There is an opportunity to discover some of the elements which may cause difficulty in relationships.

As a counsellor influenced by Klein, I sometimes find it appropriate to work with the transference and sometimes not. In a short series of consultations about the onset of an illness, it may not be appropriate to talk much about the transference, though if the person clearly has strong feelings about other people who do not have their troubles, it might be important to take this up. In the following long-term case the counsellor did pick up a transference hint.

A client was talking about how she hated other people being able to walk in the park with their children when she couldn't. Her strong feelings of envy towards other people and the distress caused by this had already been acknowledged and explored. Given the context, the counsellor took it up with her both in terms of her hatred of the counsellor being able to do this with her children (in the client's phantasy) and of her hatred of the counsellor being able to offer some kind of 'mothering' to the client when the client felt she couldn't 'mother' anyone, including her own daughter.

Counter-transference Paula Heimann's paper 'On Counter-transference' (1950) states clearly an important part of the now-accepted Kleinian view of counter-transference. It raises issues which are very much alive within the counselling world today.

Heimann describes her student's belief that counter-transference is nothing but a source of trouble. She then points out that there are two uses for the term 'counter-transference'. It is used to denote the analyst's 'transference' feelings towards the patient: feelings which arise from the analyst's own past and from the analyst's own relationships with his or her parents. Heimann is clear that this is important and that it is a factor which analysts have to take into account. However, she points out that not everything a patient feels towards his or her analyst is transference and that not everything an analyst feels towards his or her patient is the analyst's own transference.

As far as Heimann is concerned, 'the analyst's emotional response to his patient within the analytic situation represents one of the most important tools for his work. The analyst's counter-transference is *an instrument of research into the patient's unconscious*.' (Heimann, 1950: 81) (emphasis added)

What distinguishes the relationship between patient and analyst from other relationships is not the absence of feeling in one and its presence in others, but the way these feelings are experienced and the use made of them. The analyst's own analysis should enable the analyst to experience and 'sustain' the feelings aroused. In the analysis the analyst is to *reflect upon* these feelings and use them to understand the patient, not simply to react to them, to express them or to 'discharge' them.

> In my view Freud's demand that the analyst must 'recognise and master' his counter-transference does not lead to the conclusion that the counter-transference is a disturbing factor and that the analyst should become unfeeling and detached, but that he must use his emotional response as a key to the patient's unconscious. This will protect him from entering as a co-actor on the scene which the patient re-enacts in the analytic relationship and from exploiting it for his own needs. At the same time he will find ample stimulus for taking himself to task again and again and for continuing the analysis of his own problems. This, however is his private affair, and I do not consider it right for the analyst to communicate his feelings to his patient. In my view such honesty is more in the nature of a confession and a burden to the patient. In any case it leads away from the analysis. The emotions roused in the analyst will be of value to his patient, if used as one more source of insight into the patient's unconscious conflicts and defences; and when these are interpreted and worked through, the ensuing changes in the patient's ego include the strengthening of his reality sense

so that he sees his analyst as a human being, not a god or demon, and the 'human' relationship in the analytic situation follows without the analyst's having recourse to extra-analytical means. (Heimann, 1950: 83)

Hanna Segal, writing of counter-transference in *The Work of Hanna Segal*, puts it succinctly:

I had a patient who evoked in me a whole gamut of unpleasant feelings. It would have been very foolish of me to ignore these feelings or consider them my own neurotic reactions, since this patient's principal complaint was her terrible unpopularity. Obviously, the way she affected me was a function of her psychopathology – a function of utmost importance to her, and one which it is crucial for us to understand. (H. Segal, 1981: 81)

Klein did not approve of the use of counter-transference in this way. She felt that the analyst's feelings towards the patient should always be treated by the analyst as signs of the analyst's own pathology. She was disturbed at the idea of students using this concept as an excuse for avoiding unpleasant thoughts about themselves. This is illustrated by a story Segal relates. On one occasion a student was telling Klein in a seminar how he had interpreted that the patient had projected his confusion into the analyst. Klein said sharply, 'No dear, you were confused.'

The question to ask is 'What does the client make me feel?' (An answer might be, 'incompetent'.) Once an answer has been formulated, it needs to be addressed in three ways. The first is to ask whether it is a true reflection of reality. (Am I being incompetent in some way with this client?) This question might be taken up with the supervisor. The second is to ask where in the therapist it comes from. (Does this patient remind me of someone who used to make me feel incompetent? What do I feel about being incompetent? Am I using it as a defence against feeling something more dangerous, such as clever?) These researches should not be shared with the client but may be taken up in the therapist's own therapy.

The third question is to ask whether there is any way it might also be the client's feeling: a feeling the client cannot bear in themselves and which they evoke in others. (Does the client have reason to feel incompetent and difficulty feeling it? Is the client evoking this feeling in others, not just their therapist?) The ramifications of this may be explored sympathetically with the client, both in terms of the client's relations with others and in terms of his or her feelings about him/herself.

To give an illustration: a woman was talking about her newly diagnosed illness and saying how badly it was affecting her. The counsellor began to feel extremely uncomfortable, and not for the first time found herself not believing the client at all. She felt that by saying nothing she was pretending she did believe her. After a time she was able to say 'There's something strange going on. Listening to you I get a strong feeling that what you're saying is not true, and yet I know that it is. I wonder if you want me to feel it's not true so somewhere you won't have to believe it, though at the same time it is true and you are afraid I won't believe it – so you exaggerate it to make me believe it . . . If you're doing that with other people you may be having difficulty with them. They won't believe you and you're left on your own with them pretending and you feeling guilty because you feel you're making it up . . . But maybe you'd rather feel you're making it up than that it's true . . . .' This is not a model of a clear, simple intervention. It was a tentative struggle to make some sense out of a very painful situation and was presented as such. However, the client did recognise that something of this was indeed going on. In subsequent sessions she and the counsellor were able to register whenever she 'laid it on thick', and she began to detect herself doing it outside too. By the time she stopped counselling she was no longer doing it but was more able to be direct and straightforward about her symptoms.

Working with the relationship with the therapist like this gives clients a chance to look at the multiplicity of ways they communicate with others. In the process they learn about themselves as they take back inside those aspects of themselves which they previously simply ejected into others. This young woman was able to take back from the counsellor an ability to distinguish between truth and falsehood which she had so effectively deposited in the counsellor. She learnt to notice whether she was 'laying it on thick', where previously she had discarded this knowledge. The counsellor had helped her to bear the pain of acknowledging the reality of her illness on a more realistic basis and she no longer tried to circumvent it by such convoluted means.

Therapy for the Therapist
This view of counter-transference, and the importance attached to the relationship between client and therapist, makes it clear why Kleinian therapists are anxious that counsellors and other psychotherapists should have their own therapy. Without their own therapy, therapists may be more likely to react to the clients just as people have in the client's past rather than being able to hold the feelings and reflect upon them. Therapists like anyone else have difficulties with certain feelings and may use certain mechanisms to

defend themselves from the impact of a relationship; therapy for the therapist goes some way towards helping them to reduce the areas of their own personality which do not function well and so increase their sensitivity to and understanding of the client.

In particular, a therapist's own therapy enables him or her to experience the mixed feelings of being 'cared for' and dependent rather than being the 'carer' and apparently 'independent'. This can enormously increase a therapist's understanding of the process from the point of view of the client. It gives the therapist some insight into the difficulties of being the 'helped' person, where many therapists may seek out the work in order to have the pleasures of being the 'helper'. The main risk with a therapist who has not been in therapy is that some of his or her own difficulties may be evoked in the client and maintained there by the therapist for the therapist's own purposes.

The Content of Psychotherapy

Klein's work also has implications for the content of psychotherapy and counselling as practised today.

The Task

Klein saw the task of the therapist as the resolution of unconscious anxiety. When patients experienced previously unconscious feelings in analysis, the thoughts and anxieties attached to them could be shared with the analyst and in this process modified, thus changing the feelings. The feeling of danger attached to acknowledging them was reduced. She saw this as strengthening the ego through reducing the need of the patient to split off aspects of the self and attribute these to others, including the super-ego (the conscience or critical internal parents).

From a practical point of view Kleinians, like many other therapists, emphasise the importance of listening to a client with serious attention. The basic function of the therapist is to offer understanding, holding and acknowledgement of the complex feelings and anxieties brought by the client. As Bion (1967) put it, the significant question is *what* is going on: this takes priority over questions of *why*.

A full acknowledgement of internal and external reality discloses not only sadistic aspects of the self but also equally powerful empathy for others, and the desire to protect and make reparation. Therapy which uncovers 'cans of worms' will therefore also liberate the desire and the means to make something good out of them.

Interpretation

The issue of interpretation is an area where analytical therapists and others may differ. This is connected to a belief in unconscious processes but it also relates to matters of technique.

A therapist may be fairly certain that a client has feelings that he or she is not expressing; the therapist may be sure that the client is aware of these feelings and actually lying, or he or she may suspect the existence of feelings of which the client has no conscious awareness. For some people the whole idea of 'unconscious feelings' is a contradiction in terms: Freud was aware that this was a problem and yet he (and many others) were convinced that there are such things. Jane Austen in *Pride and Prejudice*, for example, makes it clear to the reader that Elizabeth is in love with Darcy well before Elizabeth recognises it herself.

However, some counsellors and therapists are very wary of pointing out to a client that they may have feelings of which they are not aware, and there is good reason for this. The dangers of telling someone they are feeling something when they are not aware of it are many. Early on, Elizabeth would have denied vehemently anything other than contempt for Darcy. She might well have felt insulted, angry and misunderstood if these contemptuous feelings were dismissed as a cover-up for an attraction. Some of the suspicion towards analytically influenced therapists of all kinds perhaps arises out of clumsy attempts to make such unconscious feelings conscious. The therapist can appear to be arrogant, 'I-know-better-than-you', and totally to misunderstand the patient or client.

Used properly, Klein's emphasis on conflict and conflicting aspects of the personality can help to reduce this kind of behaviour. The reality of the more superficial feelings can be acknowledged, while the possibility of hidden ones is also raised. Elizabeth's contempt for Darcy could have been explored until it became clear to her that she had other feelings too. The therapist needs to keep an open mind as to what these other feelings may be, without jumping to conclusions on insufficient evidence. Only when sufficient evidence *from the client* is available is it ever useful for the therapist to make the final connection: the risk that it might be the therapist's own feelings which are being interpreted is real. The sense of being invaded, controlled and unfairly judged by a wrong interpretation of unconscious feelings is very strong. The difficulty is that people can feel like this about correct interpretations too.

In five-times-a-week analysis, interpretations can be made more accurately and perhaps with less risk than in once-a-week therapy or counselling. Not only does the therapist have a better chance of

really understanding the patient, but in addition, the opportunity
to correct misunderstandings and mistakes is available sooner.

Idealisation as a Defence Against Persecution

Klein made it clear that idealisation is a defence, not against
reality, but against very persecutory phantasies. This has very practical effects in counselling. Where other therapists might not want
to disturb a very positive attitude of a client, a Kleinian would be
concerned to discover whether this attitude covered disturbing and
unrealistic fears, as in the following case.

> A woman came for counselling because she had just been
> diagnosed with an incurable illness. She was brightly cheerful
> and said how important it was to be positive. She said she
> knew she was going to be all right. The counsellor smiled and
> asked if this was real or whether she was pretending in order
> to convince herself. The woman relaxed and laughed and
> went on to talk about her aunt who had had the same illness.
> This aunt had been quite hopeless and bad-tempered. She had
> deteriorated quickly and had died young. The counsellor
> wondered aloud if she was terrified to even think about being
> bad-tempered or hopeless for fear it would mean she would
> deteriorate quickly and die young. This would make it very
> hard whenever she felt a bit depressed or irritable or anxious.
> The woman agreed and together she and the counsellor were
> able to explore how realistic her fear was. By the end of the
> session the client's fear of being depressed or angry seemed to
> have reduced. Allowing herself to feel 'bad' feelings would
> make it easier for her to think realistically even if this meant
> she had to grieve about real losses.

Trying always to 'think positively' as a defence against 'negative'
thoughts gives an air of desperation as well as superficiality and
unreality. People have to work very hard to maintain the illusion
that everything is all right. In covering up their fears about what
they have lost they cannot tell how far these losses go and where
they end. Uncovering the feared thoughts enables clients to be
more realistic about their situation and considerably reduces their
anxiety *even when the uncovered thoughts are uncomfortable*. The
known feels less threatening than the unknown. In addition, it
becomes possible to explore the real strengths and supports which
remain.

Uncovering the anxieties which lie behind an insistence on
'thinking positively' can be frightening for the therapist at first.
There are two kinds of anxiety which might be revealed. One

would be realistic; once it has been spoken it becomes something which can be acknowledged and which may be a source of grief or a cause for painful feelings of some kind. The counsellor has to sit with the client while they feel these feelings and is likely to suffer with the client's distress.

The other kind of anxiety is the extra which is added from unrealistic phantasies of doom and destruction, abandonment and disintegration, which are hidden in the unconscious of all of us, waiting for a real-life anxiety to which they can attach themselves. If any of this kind of anxiety can be reached there is a real chance of directly modifying the feelings attached to the real event or situation. The sense of being abandoned and alone which arises with any loss is already reduced to some extent if the client can be helped to share his or her anxiety with the counsellor. The guilty or miserable or terrifying secret is no longer the worse for being hidden and secret.

Speech and Symbolism
Understanding the symbolism of the patient's communications, not only through dreams, has been an essential aspect of psycho-analytic therapy since Freud wrote the *Interpretation of Dreams*. It may also play an important part in counselling. Some of the more dramatic developments in Kleinian theory since Klein's death have involved a deeper understanding of the role of symbolism. It is only possible to sketch in some of these ideas here.

Wilfred Bion maintained that phantasies deriving from the nipple were used not only to understand penises and ultimately men but also to give meaning and 'body' to words and speech. These, like the nipple, are experienced as the link between mother and child; between a source of goodness, the breast, and the child who needs it. Words both bring mother and child together and also illustrate the separation and difference between them. The fact of needing to speak implies that mother and baby are not one, indivisible, inside each other and knowing each other's mind. This makes the baby angry at times, just as an adult may get angry at the fact that they need to tell their partner what they are thinking; that they cannot communicate perfectly on a non-verbal basis. A relationship of perfect understanding with no need for words is quite clearly ideal: many adults continue to search for it in the belief that it can exist.

Understanding is felt to belong to the containing breast: the nipple provides the template for words which link it to the baby. Bion found that attacks on linking of all kinds, including words, understanding and the relationship between analyst and patient were extremely important and could be modified by analysis (Bion, 1967).

Bion took up Klein's discovery that words can have a very concrete reality. For some clients in some situations it is useful to recognise the fact that words are not clearly distinguished from things. Their magical power to create and destroy may have at times to be discussed, particularly before very frightening thoughts can be brought into the light of day.

Hanna Segal's distinction between symbolic equations and symbolic representation, or symbolism proper, is useful when looking at the meaning of speech. In a symbolic equation, the symbol is felt to *be* the thing symbolised; in symbolic representation the distinction between symbol and symbolised is acknowledged. 'If I say it it will be true' is an expression of belief in a symbolic equation: the ability to think without fearing the consequences may depend on awareness of the distinction between symbolic thoughts and whatever they symbolise. A word which is felt to be the same as the thing it represents may not be spoken freely. Sexual words sometimes have such a connotation in ordinary life: the power of swearing may be related to it.

Symbolic equations belong to the paranoid-schizoid position; symbolism proper arises in the depressive position as a means of dealing with conflicts by shifting meaning to a representative without destroying the meaning entirely. Hitting a pillow instead of one's mother depends on an ability to allow the pillow to represent her without being confused into thinking she is really about to be hurt by the blow.

A symbol is not always a word. For some men, loss of potency (through illness, for example) seems to be *the same as* loss of respect in society, loss of the ability to be a man, and impotence in a wider sense: resultant changes in behaviour may create these losses in a real sense. For other men the meaning is more clearly 'just' symbolic and more easily challenged and overcome. Any serious loss may be felt to mean 'the end of everything': but examining the nature of this belief and distinguishing carefully between losses which are concrete and losses which are symbolic may bring about significant change.

Symbolism is ever present and in any form is important: it is a way in which life is given meaning, adding to pleasures as well as to unrealistic fears. Symbolic equations may make life very much harder than it needs to be but may be modified as part of a mourning process.

The Client's Relation with Themselves

The idea that there are many different 'selves' or 'parts of us' inside us is one which can make sense to people in counselling as well as therapy. Kleinian analysts have described how one part of the self can be jealous or envious of another, so that one part might want therapy and help and another be scornful or denigrating towards it; one part be loving and hopeful and this part have to struggle with another part of the self which is hopeless and full of hate and envy (Spillius, 1988).

The mechanism of projection derives from the phantasy that people can put parts of themselves which they do not want to contain into other people. A counsellor may be able to help a client to undo the more superficial forms of projection, so increasing the client's acceptance of parts of themselves and improving their relations with those around them.

The idea that the therapist can support the client in his or her struggle with disliked aspects of him/herself is also strong in Freud – for example, in the 'Dora' case history ('Fragment of an Analysis of a Case of Hysteria': Freud, 1975, vol. VII). It lends itself to counselling practice as well as analysis:

> The problem is that you hate everyone else being all right when you aren't: and it's awful because it makes you try to spoil their pleasure and then you feel bad because of that, and you feel guilty and worthless too. And it feels as if there's no way out: all we can do is to sit here and point out how dreadful it all is . . . If I'm any good as a counsellor you hate me too, but if I'm not you've got no help at all.

The client did learn to control her envious attacks on others and she left counselling after several years saying how she felt she was losing a friend.

The Containing Function

Parents and other adults by their existence, behaviour and emotions may modify children's impulses or they may reinforce them. By holding boundaries, while acknowledging feelings, they may represent and hold not only the child's aggression, cruelty and sadism, but also the child's ability to love and create, to be fair and reasonable, to feed and care. An important aspect of therapy is that the counsellor or therapist can fulfil various aspects of the 'containing' function for their clients or patients.

In *Second Thoughts*, Bion describes the containing function:

> As a realistic activity [projective identification] shows itself as behaviour reasonably calculated to arouse in the mother feelings of which the infant wants to be rid. If the infant fears it is dying it can arouse fears that it is dying in the mother. A well-balanced mother can accept these and respond therapeutically: that is to say in a manner that makes the infant feel it is receiving its frightened personality back again but in a

form that it can tolerate – the fears are manageable by the infant personality. (Bion, 1967: 114)

A counsellor or psychotherapist who can tolerate his or her client's emotional pain performs a similar function. By her existence a mother becomes a container for the baby's unbearable experiences, including feelings which the baby cannot hold at the time. Sometimes she puts names to the painful experience: names which have meaning, such as 'You need a feed' or 'You need a clean nappy.' So too a therapist may help a client to name their experience: 'You're saying you don't like yourself when you are angry?' Or 'What you are saying is that you want someone to take all the pain away and make it all right?' By keeping the boundaries of the therapy firm, the therapist is also holding important aspects of the client's desire to work with the therapist.

Under good circumstances, the infant in phantasy takes in the mother with her ability to contain the baby's distress and to make good sense of it. A client similarly takes in a containing therapist and may refer to the therapist in their mind outside sessions. Once the child or client has a sense of someone with this containing function within, the capacity for thought and for tolerating bad feelings is increased. This breast/mother/therapist is not simply smashed to pieces by bad feelings or turned bad itself but can bear the bad experience and change it into a valuable experience, something like good food. The ability to hold and contain sense without simply evacuating it into someone else has then been taken in. A sense of space and time is created; experience does not have to be rejected or incorporated immediately but can be held for a while. Thoughts and thinking become possible. A counsellor or therapist may help a client to regain or extend his or her ability to hold experience and thus to think.

Alpha and Beta Elements

Bion brought many new ideas (and reworking of old ones) to psychoanalysis. One of his important distinctions is between 'alpha elements' and 'beta elements' in the psyche.

According to Bion, there is a function in the psyche which operates to transform sense impressions of all kinds (images, emotions, sensations, sounds) from raw, undigested material into 'alpha elements'. Alpha elements can be used for dreaming and thinking and can be stored and forgotten in a normal way. Beta elements are 'accretions of stimuli' which can be ejected, got rid of into other people or re-experienced. Under normal circumstances, the mother takes in such beta-element projections from the child at the very beginning of life, modifies them and gives them back 'predigested' and digestible for the baby. In the baby's phantasy she does this for all its unwanted excreta: faeces, urine, painful wind are transformed by the mother into good milk, understanding and comfort.

The beta elements normally include something like fears of dying and disintegration, though once we have put words to them they are no longer beta elements, but alpha elements. If the relation with the mother is good, the baby's fear of dying can be borne, modified and in some sense known for what it is: if not, it may be increased by the mother's 'uncontaining' reaction and the baby be left with a 'nameless dread': nameless because it has not been converted into something which can be named, thought about or even dreamed. The mother may be quite unaware that this is going on and may simply find she has to cope with a very difficult baby with no understanding of the problem.

This theory helps to make sense of the way people behave in psychotic states. Bion says that, for them, the alpha-function has broken down (or been destroyed); they cannot sleep or store sense impressions; they also cannot wake up and make contact with reality. In this state internal objects and external ones are perceived as the same, which is partly why murder and suicide may be possible. Bion gives the example of a man who 'may murder his parents and so feel free to love, because the anti-sexual internal parents are supposed by this act to have been evacuated. Such an act is intended "to rid the psyche of accretions of stimuli"' (Bion, 1962: 7).

This theory is also useful in thinking about counselling and what it can do. A counsellor or therapist can sometimes take in frightening sense elements from the client and enable the client to convert them into thoughts and words. 'I've never spoken of this before' is a sign that a particular kind of symbolisation is taking place for the first time. Feelings which previously were only available to be evoked in someone else may be named; this is why it is so important for counsellors and therapists to learn to put words to 'what is happening between us' because it is in this relationship that the nameless beta elements are active.

A woman left her husband and two daughters aged 5 and 7. Her own mother had done the same to her and she was puzzled because she had always said she could never do this to her children. Using Bion's theory of beta elements, we can suggest that perhaps some of the feelings aroused by the loss of her mother were never worked through into alpha elements where they could become part of her acknowledged experience. They could have remained in a 'psychotic pocket', cut off from normal awareness, waiting until they could find some way to be ejected. Her own children reaching the age she was at the time perhaps gave these beta elements an opportunity. Her children could have the feelings and she could be rid of them. Without these feelings she, like Bion's patient, perhaps also felt free to love again. Unfortunately, this solution is only temporary for the mother and in addition, it involves a severe attack on her children.

Experience with adults who have been abandoned as children by parental illness, death or divorce does suggest that they are often unaware of some of the more violent feelings which must have accompanied this abandonment: 'No, I'm not angry with her'; 'I didn't miss him.' Bion's work implies that some of these most painful feelings cannot be felt without the help of a good container, a loving adult who can help to transform them. They may later be experienced in a relationship with a partner, split off from the mother or father where they originally belonged: 'My wife makes me very angry.' Or, in the absence of directly sensing them, they may be evoked in others: 'My children won't miss me if I go, so I can leave.'

The beta elements are felt as dangerous objects liable to destroy those around them; their existence as feelings is not recognised. The fear of the damage they could do if allowed to emerge may prevent a child (and later, an adult) trying to express them. Children may not dare ask if a parent is going to die from an illness out of a fear that the thought itself will kill the parent. Children frequently protect their parents from knowing how hurt they are: 'I couldn't tell my mother I missed my father: she'd have been upset.'

The beta elements of any trauma will evoke past beta elements which have not been worked through. They will include the most frightening experiences the child ever experienced. They will include feelings abandoned as unbearable when the adult was a tiny baby. They will include something like the experience of being abandoned at a very young age, left not with an absent mother but with a present dangerous and cruel witch-like person: something considerably more monstrous than the 'burglar under the bed' of children's night fears. It is not surprising that adults do not encourage children to express such terrible feelings, by definition actually unimaginable. Our language makes it clear that we know of these things. The unimaginable is infinitely worse than the imaginable.

Without help expressing these unimaginable feelings, the children themselves cannot locate and know them. They are left not knowing what they feel; perhaps with a sense of something missing, of a gap. They may have a sense of a desperate need to fill it with something, but with something that will not be exactly what is required. These undigested beta elements may contribute to eating and learning difficulties, where what is taken in is never right, never satisfying and can never be fully enjoyed.

Violent sexual experiences give rise to beta-element traumas which may be re-experienced in the transference. Clients who have been raped or otherwise abused may feel that they are being raped or abused, if only verbally, by the counsellor or therapist. In these situations the only option seems to be to work with the transference since the anxieties evoked will otherwise be too strong for the therapy to hold.

Working with Psychoses

Some organisations which work with people who suffer from psychoses are interested in the insights of Klein and her successors. The Richmond Fellowship, the Arbours (in London) and Mind (Hammersmith, London), for example, have all taught Kleinian ideas to their workers to enable them to work better with clients.

In psychoses, the relation of the self with reality is extremely disturbed. Bion found that the perceptual apparatus – hearing, seeing, thinking – was itself under attack. Where a 'neurotic' response to seeing something which is not liked may be to turn away or to look somewhere else, the psychotic response is to attack the processes of perception: of seeing, hearing or perceiving one's own thoughts and feelings. One way in which this can happen is that the ability to see or hear or feel is projected: the person may hallucinate eyes looking at them, or imagine that a record player is listening to them. They may go temporarily blind or deaf. Parts of the self may also be projected in a way which becomes very frightening: one man described himself as pouring himself into a small bottle on the table.

Bion thought that for some people the only way in which things could come together was in a cruel and destructive way. He thought that there was a serious disturbance at the level of the link between the baby and the mother. The feeding situation somehow became infused with cruelty or hypocrisy, where goodness was simply seen as a pretence to cover extreme cruelty.

In this situation the early processes of splitting do not happen properly, so the child is left with a muddle between good and bad, nice and nasty, love and cruelty. Some disturbed adults show this muddling very clearly, for example, when they fear (groundlessly) that their food is poisoned. Adults and children sometimes react to good and loving behaviour as if it were an attack, just as the baby can turn on the nipple as if it were an attacker.

Watching some mothers with their babies it also seems that babies can be exposed to circumstances in which feeding is always accompanied by some subtle kind of cruelty; such children may well grow up disturbed and seeking or creating cruel relationships. This may arise for reasons to do with the mother's inability to cope with the baby's attacking impulses, to contain them successfully and give them back in a manageable form. This may be because she has difficulty handling her own conscious or unconscious cruelty, or it may arise because the baby has particularly strong needs which this particular mother cannot at this particular time handle, though at other times she can or could. Equally, the difficulty may arise from something inborn in the child which prevents the child using good parenting offered to them. There may be a combination of these factors and others we do not understand.

The work of the Kleinians in many contexts has made it clear how much the 'normal' personality includes psychotic areas of functioning: areas cut off from contact with reality, either internal or external. Those who work with people who have psychoses may find the psychotic aspects of their own personality resonating: this can be very disturbing.

Bion made it very clear that he considered there was a sane part of the personality in people even when they appear mad. He thought it was very important to remember this and to speak to this part of the personality, even when under great pressure to pretend that it does not exist.

The difficulty for this sane part of the person is that if they acknowledge it they have to recognise that they are mad: if they ignore it and deny it their madness has succeeded in destroying it. People working with people diagnosed as schizophrenic, for example, may be under great pressure to believe the crazy ideas being put to them. If they go along with these they have joined in the phantasy that not only the mad person is mad but also the sane ones have become mad. This can be very frightening. Part of the difficulty for such staff is their own fears of the mad person's envy; if they are sane, will they not be attacked all the more? They might, but this may be preferable in the long term to the hopelessness of the phantasy that no sanity exists that can withstand the madness.

A young man in a hostel for mentally disturbed people was screaming that the place was mad, he had to get out because it was driving him mad. He was obviously really terrified and apparently quite out of control, trying to hide from the staff who wanted to calm him and couldn't. The warden arrived and spoke to him in a matter-of-fact way. 'No,' he said, 'I'm not mad, we're not mad; you are.' The young man calmed down and did not need to be sent to hospital.

It seems that the warden had succeeded in talking to the sane part of the young man. Once he knew someone could recognise his madness and distinguish it from sanity the young man no longer needed to project it into the building and all the people in it: thus he could feel safer in a less mad environment. The warden may well have represented to him his sane self which could see his madness: he could take this from the warden and regain a more sane view of the rest of the world. The warden had succeeded in showing him that sanity could survive the young man's attacks: that understanding and containment was possible without cruelty.

The other staff were astonished: they said they would never have dared to say straightforwardly to anyone that they were mad. Their feelings probably reflected not only 'normal' reactions to madness but also some of the conflicting feelings of the young man. His sense of the danger of seeing how mad he was was probably one of the determinants in his attributing it to the building and the other people. It is clear that the paradoxes for those who confuse sanity and madness, cruelty and kindness, affectionate relationships with attacking, are very distressing and painful.

P.L.G. Gallwey, a Kleinian analyst who has worked extensively with criminals, has described (in an unpublished lecture) sudden murderous attacks by people who previously showed no disturbance as also perhaps arising from a split-off 'psychotic pocket' which for some reason is suddenly activated.

Staff in a hostel for psychotically disturbed people found that some of the ideas of Klein and Bion on schizophrenia and psychosis were enormously helpful. The natural way of judging whether we or our behaviour are good or bad is by the response we get: the work of Klein and Bion makes it clear that the responses of people who are psychotic may be exactly the opposite of those expected. They may respond very negatively to behaviour felt to be good and sane because it arouses such terrible envy of the sanity and goodness of the other person. Equally, a resident on one level may be happy when a staff member behaves in a mad or destructive way: this 'proves' that the staff member has nothing which the resident does not have.

The realisation that staff had to judge for each other and for themselves whether their behaviour was good or bad was not a simple solution to the difficulties they faced, but at least it clarified the confusion. Their sense of being undermined, confused, driven mad and destroyed themselves became clear as at least to some extent a picking up of the resident's own unbearable feelings. This meant that they could stop trying to destroy their own minds, their own sanity and goodness and ability to live reasonably normal working lives out of a desire to avoid arousing envy in the residents.

Trauma and Disaster Work

Work with survivors of concentration camps has contributed to the psychoanalytical study of the effects of war which began with the treatment of 'shell-shock' in the First World War. This work did not impinge much on the public consciousness for many years. The Aberfan disaster in 1960, for example, did not lead to any coordinated support for those bereaved of their children in a horrifying, preventable landslip. However, more recent disasters such as that at Hillsborough football ground and the sinking of the *Herald of Free Enterprise* have mobilised interest in helping the victims to cope with the traumas involved. In the USA the publicity given to experiences of Vietnam veterans has also had an influence on public consciousness of the real and lasting effects of traumas.

Some of the work of people in these areas has been influenced by Kleinian ideas among others, but the treatment of people after traumatic events is as yet by no means satisfactory. However, in some areas the police force, fire brigade and the armed services have now begun to recognise the need for their staff to seek some kind of help in dealing with the emotional after-effects of disasters. The Tavistock Clinic Disaster Seminar has been influential here.

Working with Trauma Victims

Increasingly people have become aware that traumatic events can leave many damaging effects. There is a risk that the memories of the events will simply be cut off from awareness and remain in 'psychotic pockets' in the psyche, unassimilated and very frightening, ready to be reactivated by the next fear or to emerge as nightmares or disturbing symptoms.

Bion's distinction between experiences which can be symbolised, dreamt about and used in creative acts, and experiences which can only be ejected, relived or re-experienced is very important here. Work is now sometimes done to help people who have been through traumatic events to symbolise their experiences by talking, drawing, writing or enacting them. This can be a very disturbing experience for the individual and for anyone listening. Terrible as it is, it is vitally important. Neglect of this process with Vietnam veterans left many totally and tragically unable to readjust to normal life after the war.

Bion's theory of alpha and beta elements helps partly to explain some of the puzzling nature of why it should be that talking through traumatic events might be helpful. The re-experiencing of the feelings in a safe situation with someone who will not judge the client harshly (as the child him or herself and his or her internal parents do) may be vital in allowing conversion of the experience from beta to alpha elements. Without this working through, the person is left vulnerable to nightmares which simply bring the feelings back, unmodified, or to serious disturbances of behaviour and relationships.

A naval officer described an experience in which his life was at serious risk for several hours twenty years previously. He had never spoken to anyone about it. The trauma was still appearing in nightmares; he would sometimes attack his wife in bed in a half-waking state. He was still angry with his superior officer for failing to support him at the time and for never giving him an opportunity to discuss what had happened. He felt bitterly let down by what he interpreted as a rejection of his distress by his superior. He was quite explicit that a parent-figure was required who could make sense of the experience; someone who could make it thinkable and bearable. Without this help, he had simply taken it out on his wife who had no idea what was happening. She was made to feel the confusion, anger, despair, abandonment and terror for his life which was part of her husband's original trauma.

The danger, of course, is that people like this (and there are many in numerous occupations) may move on to traumatise others. Not only are they likely to abandon the men or women in their charge if they are promoted, but they may also be tempted to create in members of the public the feelings they have suffered. Some of the ill-treatment of petty criminals in Britain, for example, may arise from policemen's or prison officers' attempts to get rid of such beta elements into somebody else in a situation where the person cannot retaliate.

Clearly, these reactions are well known. We are talking about 'taking it out on' someone, commonly known as 'kicking the cat'. But Bion makes some important points about when and why this happens. The immediate 'kicking the cat' reaction to a bad day at work may be a way of getting rid of a feeling which cannot be borne, but it may also perform a less negative function. However unpleasant, it may provide an opportunity to think, to feel guilty, to locate the difficulties and to convert them into thoughts and recognisable sense impressions: to pay attention to them.

The difficulty with more traumatic situations is that this cannot be done. The cat is unlikely to be kicked in the immediate aftermath; the person is in a state of shock and withdrawal, probably not making contact with the world around at all: attempting to cut off sense impressions rather than to symbolise or express them. The threat to the sense of the coherence of the self is huge: the mind has been flooded with emotions and reactions which seriously threaten the sense of the self as a good, loving person. Willingness to kill others to survive, for example, is a shocking feeling to discover: so too is the excitement and pleasure of total fear, and the way in which people around are in such circumstances not perceived as people but as things or comic-strip enemies.

In these situations, sharing and talking through the feelings with people who were there may be very helpful. Counselling may enable beta elements to be transformed into alpha elements. For this to happen, the client has to trust that the counsellor will not themselves be damaged. At this point the feelings are felt as extremely dangerous objects, terrifying things, and the belief that they will actually damage the counsellor is likely to be very strong. Some workers insist that the counsellor should already have undergone such an experience: there are many good conscious reasons for this demand. One unconscious motivation may be that a counsellor who has already experienced these feelings may be seen (along with other participants in the disaster) as damaged already, so the guilt of throwing the experience at the counsellor may be reduced.

The feelings evoked by a trauma such as a disaster or torture are difficult to digest and the therapist needs to obtain help themselves to 'digest' them, if he or she is not to fail the client. Just as a mother needs mothering at the time she gives birth, if the baby's most disturbing phantasies are to be contained by her, so therapists dealing with traumas need good and supportive supervision and/or therapy if they are to be able to contain the truly terrifying and monstrous anxieties of traumatised clients. The contribution of therapists who themselves have been through traumatic situations may be of great value here: it is extremely important that they should obtain good supervisory support and therapy themselves to ensure that they deal with their own unresolved psychotic anxieties without inflicting them on clients.

Grief Work

Part of the more general influence of Klein has been on attitudes to grief and mourning. Klein was very clear that depressive feelings were a sign of work being done and, as such, not to be ignored or rejected. She described the initial manic defences against grief and connected maturity and development with the ability to tolerate the pain of loss. Loss of real, loved people begins a process in which the self takes over some of their characteristics and then gradually sorts out which belong to the other person and are painfully lost, and which belong to the self and can be kept. The potential collapse of the internal object and temporary loss of identity resulting from a significant loss were also described by Klein.

People are also beginning to recognise that one loss evokes another, and that the effect of one loss depends on those which went before. The length of time which it takes to work through a loss of a loved person is more acknowledged, as well as the inadvisability of attempting to cut short a grieving process.

Work with Organisations, Chronic Illness and Disability

Isabel Menzies and Elliot Jacques are Kleinian analysts who have sought ways to humanise organisations using many of Klein's ideas. Consultancy work with organisations such as hospitals, schools, prisons and many others is often influenced by their ideas (see Menzies-Lyth, 1988; Jacques in Klein et al., 1955). J. Segal (1991a) is a recent paper influenced by their work.

Since 1985 I have been working as Research Counsellor for Action and Research for Multiple Sclerosis, counselling people with multiple sclerosis (MS), members of their families and professionals involved with them. In this work I have drawn extensively on the work of Klein and her pupils. The insights of Klein help to make sense of the effects of illness and disability on the lives of those who come into contact with them. The importance of the symbolism attributed to the illness by each individual concerned and the way this can threaten existing defence mechanisms and appear to confirm or disprove significant phantasies have provided a rich source of insight, enabling people to disentangle some of the real and unavoidable effects of their condition from phantasised or avoidable ones (J. Segal, 1989, 1991b).

Following hints from the work of Menzies-Lyth, the influence on professionals of working with MS has also proved a valuable area of research. The idea, deriving from the concept of projective identification, that professionals working with a particular condition might show signs of similar difficulties to those of their clients, is a powerful one. It has been used to help many professionals to look differently at the relation between themselves and their clients, to understand and break down some of the divisions between 'them and us', for example. Attitudes to dependence, independence and control, also of significance in illness, can be challenged and enriched with the ideas of Klein and her pupils (J. Segal, 1987).

Klein's Influence on Influential Theorists

Winnicott and Bowlby

Many counsellors and therapists have been influenced by the work of Winnicott and Bowlby. Although eventually there were strong disagreements between them and Klein, some of which were discussed in Chapter 4, many of their ideas were based on her work. Their work was significant in disseminating ideas to the general public about the importance of maintaining children's earliest relationships with a mother-figure. The dangers of depriving children of someone who loves them and cares about them as well as for them have been recognised. Hospital, social work and childcare practices have been affected to some extent as a result. Children are no longer officially supposed to be treated as if it made no difference to them whether they were looked after by one person or many, though the emotional care of children (and adults) in hospital and in other institutional settings (such as women's prisons) still leaves much to be desired.

The work of Bowlby has been criticised, and in many ways rightly, but he did emphasise the importance and value to a child of even a 'bad' mother, and began to challenge the too-easy and damaging removal of children from their parents. Bowlby became more interested in the measurable effects of external events and relationships on children than on the workings of their minds. His work has been very significant in changing childcare practices but many analysts, including Winnicott, feel that it moved away from analysis. Bowlby himself readily acknowledges his roots in Klein's theories though he disagreed more and more with her over the issue of the relative importance of internal processes and external influences on children.

Lacan, Laing and the Women's Movement

R.D. Laing and the French analyst Lacan both claimed that they owed Klein a great debt, though she and her students did not approve of their work. Laing's writing on schizophrenia seems to idealise it and to underestimate the extreme suffering of the person with the condition. However, his work has led some people to seek out Klein and other Kleinians and to work directly and sympathetically with people suffering from various psychoses.

Lacan was eventually expelled from the International Psychoanalytical Association and set up his own branch of the French Psychoanalytical Society. He too was responsible for publicising the ideas of Klein: like Laing, he became for a time a cult figure amongst people who wanted to challenge the ruling ideologies. Lacan wrote in a way which is extremely (and intentionally) mystifying. In his writings he idealises the phallus (conscious and unconscious fantasies of the penis); in spite of this he was adopted as a guru by a group of British radical feminists in the mid-1970s. Juliet Mitchell, a member of this group, wrote about him in her book *Psychoanalysis and Feminism* (1975) which challenged the American feminist view that Freud and psychoanalysis had nothing to teach women. Bizarre as it seems, Lacan's squabbles with the international psychoanalytical community did lead to psychoanalysis becoming a respectable subject among radical feminists in the mid-1970s.

It was not until 1976, at a conference on patriarchy inspired by the work of Lacan, that psychoanalysis was discussed seriously by the Women's Movement in London. As a result of this conference, study groups on Klein and other female psychoanalysts were set up and Klein was taken more seriously by feminist theorists. *Mothering Psychoanalysis* by Janet Sayers (1991), about four women analysts, Helene Deutsch, Karen Horney, Anna Freud and Melanie Klein, was written within this context. Many of the theorists of the Women's Movement in London have since become analysts or therapists of various persuasions themselves.

Susie Orbach and her colleagues at the Women's Therapy Centre in London have worked with ideas of Klein and other analysts, increasing our understanding of women in general and eating disorders in particular. Orbach's *Fat is a Feminist Issue* (1978) describes in detail some of the unconscious phantasies women have about their bodies which influence their eating.

Writings on Klein

Book sales are one of the ways of tracing the influence of a writer. The *Introduction to the Work of Melanie Klein* by Hanna Segal (1973), which came out first in 1964, still sells. So too do the books and papers written by Klein, now published as four volumes of her writings by Virago and a selection by Penguin. In 1979 Hanna Segal's *Klein* was published, the first woman in the Fontana

Modern Masters series. There is now an extensive literature based on the work of Klein, listed in the Kleinian Reading List.

Conclusion

Melanie Klein was one of the most creative thinkers of the twentieth century. Her insights into the emotional life of children grew out of her experience as a mother enlightened by her own analysis and her reading of Freud. She has given us permission to see our children as feeling, thinking beings rather than as a bundle of instincts, responding to parents only in so far as they satisfy the child's physical needs. Babies' and children's feelings and thoughts are not the same as adults', but Klein has challenged us to consider and actually observe the ways children experience the world in phantasy.

Klein's work challenges many of the accepted ways of behaving in our society. By refusing any form of cover-up and insisting on the importance of truth, she challenges many of the current ways of relating to people in which pretence is condoned. Her insistence that truth is *more bearable* than illusion is a radical departure from tradition. The idea that it might sometimes be good for us to be upset, to grieve and to feel pain is contradictory to common beliefs.

Her views on the importance of internal conflicts challenges many of the accepted ways of treating children. Many parents believe that the way to make their children (particularly girls) grow up loving and well behaved is only to speak to them as if they were loving, kind and sweet; they often feel that the way to deal with jealousy, destructiveness, anger and sadism is to ignore it: failing to take it seriously and often even to give it a name. Klein's work makes it clear that this behaviour is likely to leave the child alone with these vital feelings unacknowledged and unrecognised or simply defined as 'bad'; it is unlikely to help them to modify and integrate these feelings into a more human character, able both to assert itself and to feel empathy.

Recognition that children bring their own difficulties to the relationship with their mothers is not a popular view. Klein does not support those who blame parents entirely for children's difficulties, while at the same time she shows how parents can be more available and supportive to their children.

In the mental health field, in particular, Klein's work has challenged the accepted distinctions between sanity and madness: demonstrating, on the one hand, the psychotic mechanisms at work in normal development and, on the other, the importance of distinguishing between mad and sane behaviour and thought. In this way her work has helped professionals to distinguish between themselves and those they work with in a way which is sympathetic, understanding and creative; neither exaggerating nor denigrating the differences and the similarities between them.

Klein's work on envy, in particular envy of female creativity, may have shocked analysts but it has provided us with a new tool for understanding some of the ways in which people of both sexes relate to women and femininity in our society.

Klein was sometimes afraid that her work would not survive her and that psychoanalysis itself was under threat. However, her influence lives on in the work of some of the most gifted of the present generation of British analysts. In addition, many of her ideas and ways of looking at the world have found resonance and development elsewhere not only amongst parents struggling with their children but also in the work of psychotherapists, counsellors, teachers, nurses, social workers and many other professionals. But there is a still a long way to go before the insights of Klein become more fully part of our society.

A Kleinian Reading List

Anderson, Robin (ed.) (1992) *Clinical Lectures on Klein and Bion*. London: Tavistock and Routledge.

Bion, Wilfred R. (1962) 'Learning from experience', in *Seven Servants: Four Works by Wilfred R. Bion* (1977). New York: Aronson.

Bion, Wilfred R. (1963) 'Elements of psychoanalysis', in *Seven Servants: Four Works by Wilfred R. Bion* (1977). New York: Aronson.

Bion, Wilfred R. (1965) 'Transformations', in *Seven Servants: Four Works by Wilfred R. Bion* (1977). New York: Aronson.

Bion, Wilfred R. (1967) *Second Thoughts*. New York: Aronson.

Bion, Wilfred R. (1970) 'Attention and interpretation', in *Seven Servants: Four Works by Wilfred R. Bion* (1977). New York: Aronson.

Britton, Ron, Feldman, Michael and O'Shaughnessy, Edna (1989) *The Oedipus Complex Today. Clinical Interpretations*. London: Karnac Books.

Grosskurth, Phyllis (1986) *Melanie Klein*. London: Hodder and Stoughton.

Heimann, Paula (1950) 'On Countertransference', *International Journal of Psycho-Analysis*, 31: 81–4.

Hinshelwood, R.D. (1991) *A Dictionary of Kleinian Thought*. London: Free Association Books.

Joseph, Betty (1989) 'Psychic equilibrium and psychic change', in E. Bott Spillius and M. Feldman (eds), *Selected Papers of Betty Joseph*. London: Tavistock/Routledge in association with the Institute of Psychoanalysis.

King, Pearl and Steiner, Riccardo (eds) (1990) *The Freud–Klein Controversies 1941–45*. London: Routledge.

Klein, Melanie (1975) *The Writings of Melanie Klein*, 4 vols. Vol. I: *Love, Guilt and Reparation and Other Works 1921–1945*. Vol. II: *The Psychoanalysis of Children*. Vol. III: *Envy and Gratitude and Other Works 1946–1963*. Vol. IV: *Narrative of a Child Analysis. The Conduct of Psycho-Analysis of Children as Seen in the Treatment of a Ten-year-old Boy*. London: Hogarth Press and the Institute of Psychoanalysis.

Klein, Melanie, Heimann, Paula, Isaacs, Susan and Riviere, Joan (eds) (1952) *Developments in Psychoanalysis*. London: Hogarth Press and the Institute of Psychoanalysis.

Klein, Melanie, Heimann, Paula and Money-Kyrle, Roger (eds) (1955/71) *New Directions in Psychoanalysis*. London: Tavistock.

Menzies-Lyth, Isabel (1988) *Containing Anxiety in Institutions. Selected Essays*. 2 vols. London: Free Association Books.

Mitchell, Juliet (ed.) (1986) *The Selected Melanie Klein*. Harmondsworth: Penguin.

Riviere, Joan (1991) *The Inner World and Joan Riviere. Collected Papers 1920–1958*, ed. Athol Hughes. London: Karnac Books.

Rosenfeld, Herbert (1965) *Psychotic States*. London: Hogarth Press and Institute of Psychoanalysis.

Segal, Hanna (1973) *Introduction to the Work of Melanie Klein*. London: Hogarth Press and the Institute of Psychoanalysis.

Segal, Hanna (1979) *Klein*. Fontana Modern Masters. Republished Brighton and London: Harvester Press.

Segal, Hanna (1981) *The Work of Hanna Segal*. New York: Aronson. Republished as *Delusion and Creativity*. London: Free Association Books, 1986.

Segal, Hanna (1985) 'The Klein–Bion Model', in Arnold Rothstein (ed.), *Models of the Mind*. New York: International Universities Press.

Segal, Hanna (1990) *Dream, Phantasy and Art*. London: Routledge.

Segal, Julia C. (1979) 'Mother, sex and envy in a children's story', *International Review of Psycho-Analysis* 6(4): 483.

Segal, Julia C. (1985) *Phantasy in Everyday Life. A Psychoanalytical Approach to Understanding Ourselves*. London: Penguin.

Segal, Julia C. (1991) 'The use of the concept of unconscious phantasy in understanding reactions to chronic illness', *Counselling*, 2(4): 146–9.

Spillius, Elizabeth Bott (ed.) (1988) *Melanie Klein Today*. Vol. I: *Mainly Theory*. Vol. II: *Mainly Practice*. London: Routledge and the Institute of Psychoanalysis.

Steiner, John (1985) 'Turning a blind eye: the cover up for Oedipus', *International Review of Psycho-Analysis*, 12(2): 161–73.

The *International Journal of Psycho-Analysis* (1983), 64(3) is devoted entirely to Melanie Klein Centenary Papers.

References

Balint, Alice (1936) 'Handhabung der Übertragung auf Grund der Ferenczischen Versuche', *Int. Zeitschr f. Psychoanal.* Vol XXII.

Bion, Wilfred (1962) *Learning from Experience*.

Bion, Wilfred R. (1967) *Second Thoughts*. New York: Aronson.

Bruch, Hilda (1974) *Eating Disorders*. London: Routledge and Kegan Paul.

Freud, Sigmund (1975) *The Standard Edition of the Complete Psychological Works of Sigmund Freud*, ed. J. Strachey. London: Hogarth Press and the Institute of Psychoanalysis, 24 vols. Some republished by Penguin.

Furman, Erna (1974) *A Child's Parent Dies*. Yale: Yale University Press.

Grosskurth, Phyllis (1986) *Melanie Klein*. London: Hodder and Stoughton.

Heimann, Paula (1950) 'On Countertransference', *International Journal of Psycho-Analysis*, 31: 81–4.

Kernberg, Otto F. (1969) 'A contribution to the ego-psychological critique of the Kleinian School', *International Journal of Psycho-Analysis*, 50: 317–33.

King, Pearl and Steiner, Riccardo (eds) (1990) *The Freud–Klein Controversies 1941–45*. London: Routledge.

Klein, Melanie (1975) *The Writings of Melanie Klein*, 4 vols. Vol. I: *Love, Guilt and Reparation and Other Works 1921–1945*. Vol. II: *The Psychoanalysis of Children*. Vol. III: *Envy and Gratitude and Other Works 1946–1963*. Vol. IV: *Narrative of a Child Analysis. The Conduct of the Psycho-Analysis of Children as Seen in the Treatment of a Ten-year-old Boy*. London: Hogarth Press and the Institute of Psychoanalysis.

Klein, Melanie, Heimann, Paula, Isaacs, Susan and Riviere, Joan (eds) (1952) *Developments in Psychoanalysis*. London: Hogarth Press and the Institute of Psychoanalysis.

Klein, Melanie, Heimann, Paula and Money-Kyrle, Roger (eds) (1955/71) *New Directions in Psychoanalysis*. London: Tavistock.

Menzies-Lyth, Isabel (1988) *Containing Anxiety in Institutions. Selected Essays*. 2 vols. London: Free Association Books.

Miller, Jonathan (1983) *States of Mind*. New York: Methuen.

Mitchell, Juliet (ed.) (1975) *Psychoanalysis and Feminism*. Harmondsworth: Penguin.

Orbach, Susie (1978) *Fat is a Feminist Issue*. London: Hamlyn.

Ramon, Shula (ed.) (1991) *Beyond Community Care*. London: Macmillan.

Rosenfeld, Herbert (1965) *Psychotic States*. London: Hogarth Press and Institute of Psychoanalysis.

Sayers, Janet (1991) *Mothering Psychoanalysis*. London: Hamish Hamilton.

Segal, Hanna (1973) *Introduction to the Work of Melanie Klein*. London: Hogarth Press and the Institute of Psychoanalysis.

Segal, Hanna (1979) *Klein*. Fontana Modern Masters. Republished Brighton and London: Harvester Press.

Segal, Hanna (1981) *The Work of Hanna Segal*. New York: Aronson. Republished as *Delusion and Creativity*. London: Free Association Books, 1986.

Segal, Hanna (1982) 'Mrs Klein as I knew her', unpublished paper read at the Tavistock Clinic Meeting to celebrate the birth of Melanie Klein, July.

Segal, Hanna (in preparation) 'The death instinct'.

Segal, Julia C. (1979) 'Mother, sex and envy in a children's story', *International Review of Psycho-Analysis*, 6(4): 483.

Segal, Julia C. (1987) 'Independence and control: issues in the counselling of people with MS', *Counselling*, 62 (November): 146-9.

Segal, Julia C. (1989) 'Counselling people with disabilities/chronic illnesses', in Windy Dryden, Ray Woolfe and David Charles-Edwards (eds), *Handbook of Counselling in Britain*. London: Tavistock/Routledge. pp. 329-46.

Segal, Julia C. (1991a) 'The professional perspective', in Shula Ramon (ed.), *Beyond Community Care*. London: Macmillan.

Segal, Julia C. (1991b) 'The use of the concept of unconscious phantasy in understanding reactions to chronic illness', *Counselling*, 2(4): 146-9.

Spillius, Elizabeth Bott (ed.) (1988) *Melanie Klein Today*, 2 vols. Vol. I: *Mainly Theory*. Vol. II: *Mainly Practice*. London: Routledge and the Institute of Psychoanalysis.

Steiner, John. (1985) 'Turning a blind eye: the cover up for Oedipus', *International Review of Psycho-Analysis*, 12(2): 161-73.

Stern, Daniel (1985) *The Interpersonal World of the Infant*. New York: Basic Books.

Tustin, Frances (1974) *Autism and Childhood Psychosis*. London: Hogarth Press.

Winnicott, D.W. (1964) *The Child, the Family and the Outside World*. London: Penguin.

Index

STAFF LIBRARY
ST. LAWRENCE'S HOSPITAL
BODMIN
PL31 2QT